THE COACH AT WORK

Copyright © The National Coaching Foundation
1986

ISBN 0 947850 22 8

First published 1986 by
The National Coaching Foundation
114 Cardigan Road, Headingley, Leeds LS6 3BJ

Reprinted 1992, 1993, 1994

Designed and produced by
White Line Publishing Services
1A Headingley Mount, Headingley, Leeds LS6 3EL
for The National Coaching Foundation

Design: Gerald Rogers
Diagrams: Stephen Beaumont
Cartoons: Bill Rudling

Typeset in 10/11 pt Garamond by H. Charlesworth
& Co. Ltd., Huddersfield

Printed and bound in Great Britain

This book is based on material written by John
Alderson, Malcolm Armstrong, John Atkinson,
Celia Brackenridge, Phyl Edwards, John Fazey, Dr
Lew Hardy, and John Shedden.

Note
Throughout this book, the pronouns "he", "him"
and "his" have been used inclusively, and are
intended to apply to both men and women. It is
important in sport, as elsewhere, that women and
men should have equal status and equal
opportunities.

NCF Coaching Handbook no. 1

THE COACH AT WORK

NATIONAL COACHING
FOUNDATION

Chapter 1
Your Coaching Philosophy

As a coach you already know what coaches do—or at least you know what *you* do when *you* are coaching. But have you stopped to think *why* you act as you do, and have you asked yourself what you really want to achieve?

It would be simple to say that as a coach you are helping others to take part in sport and to improve their performance. Many other people could make the same claim—parents, teachers, officials, equipment suppliers, sponsors—so what makes you different?

Perhaps it will help if you consider what coaching is and how it differs from the help given to performers in other ways. Coaching is not only instructing or teaching or training—it is all three and more!

COACHING = INSTRUCTION + TEACHING + TRAINING + ...

Understanding this will help you to appreciate the role you have to play more fully. Remember: raising your own standard of performance as a coach will help you to improve the standard of your performers.

Let us take a closer look at what we mean by instructing, teaching, training and coaching.

Instruction

When you instruct your performers in an activity, you are normally telling them to carry out a sequence of actions (perhaps including thought processes as well as physical acts). Effectively, you are giving them a series of predetermined commands—a kind of drill. There is an underlying assumption that you, the instructor, have the experience and knowledge to be able to predict the outcome of the learners' actions. Only if this is the case, will the learners gain competence at the activity.

Teaching

Teaching involves the communication of broad concepts. In teaching you try to show not only what these concepts are but also how to use them and develop them in different situations. Good teaching will excite and stimulate performers to make the concepts their own—and then to go on to develop them further by their own efforts.

Training

Training is concerned with acquiring and improving skilful performance, primarily by developing consistency and efficiency. This is largely a matter of guided practice. Training makes the learner adapt so that the responses become automated, thus enabling him to acquire more complex patterns of movement. In part this adaptation is physiological, involving all the body's systems, but it is also a matter of the learner developing knowledge, understanding and perception.

Training is normally related to the *desired outcome* of a given task—not just what to do, but how to do it successfully.

Coaching

Coaching is the organised provision of assistance to an individual performer or a group of performers in order to help them develop and improve in their chosen sport. Coaching therefore involves instruction, teaching and training, but it also has additional distinctive features.

Effective coaching depends on:

- intending to **maximize the potential** of the performer(s)
- recognizing the **long-term needs** of the performer or team

Substantial progress towards the full realization of individual or team potential can only be achieved on a long-term basis.

As a good coach, you should have a *code of ethics* which puts the rights and the needs of your performers before those of the sport or of yourself. You will need to develop a caring and continuing relationship with your performers. Remember, participating in sport is a socializing process, and your coaching may well shape the lives of your charges.

Why do you coach?

To clarify your coaching philosophy, first examine your objectives. Out of the many possible objectives, which of the following is the most important to you?

- to help your performer(s) or team to grow and develop as individuals
- to help them win
- to help them enjoy themselves and have fun

Perhaps it is all three—but if you have to choose, which comes first?

If you are to be a good coach, of true value to your club, performers, team and sport, you will need to take on board all three of these objectives, and not to elevate any of them too much above the others.

What do you mean by success?

Perhaps you need to consider what you mean by success. If success is only about beating others, then it can become a dangerous weapon. As a good coach you have a responsibility to keep a balanced view of participation, fair play, and—above all—justice, in the minds and behaviour of all your performers.

We all know that it is good to be successful, whereas it can be a painful experience to fail. So you as coach need to ensure that your performer always has a chance of succeeding. No, this doesn't mean rigging the competition! It means ensuring that you set each individual his own personal target—achieving a personal best; controlling that infamous temper; striving to the very end of the game; or simply enjoying the challenge. In other words, success has to be a much broader concept than simply winning or coming first.

It is your job as coach to foster the personal development of your performers and not to set unrealistic goals. If your performers are always asked to aim high, and as a consequence always fall short, then they will become despondent and disillusioned. If they need it, talk to each performer and discuss your aims and objectives with them—don't assume they have the same philosophy as you! And if their aims and objectives are different from yours, don't steam-roller over them: respect your performers. There is a much-repeated saying: *Athlete first—winning second*. There is no doubt that if you put your performers' total well-being first, you will succeed as a coach.

Chapter 2

Your Coaching Tasks

What is your job as a coach? You may see your job in different ways, depending on your situation and your approach to coaching. As Shakespeare wrote:

All the world's a stage,
And all the men and women merely players:

They have their exits and their entrances;
And one man in his time plays many parts ...

As a coach you may be asked to "play many parts"—can you? You must be capable of filling all these roles:

Instructor	directing activity
Teacher	imparting new knowledge and ideas
Motivator	producing a positive, decisive approach
Disciplinarian	setting rewards and punishments
Manager	leading and directing your performers
Administrator	dealing efficiently with the paperwork
Publicity agent	in touch with the media and the public
Social worker	counselling, advising, supporting
Friend	giving time to build a real relationship
Scientist	analysing, evaluating and drawing conclusions
Student	listening, learning, thinking for yourself

What makes you good at your job?

It would be impossible (and very foolish) to give a standard answer to this—there is no magic solution. There is certainly no substitute for knowing the techniques, rules and strategies of your sport. However, there are other things the good coach has to know. You need to understand your performers not merely as technically efficient "machines", but as people in their own right. Being able to motivate your performers and to help them cope with success and failure should not be a matter of chance or of instinct alone. You must *learn* how to guide your performers through the stress of competition and to understand their reactions and emotions. It is equally important that you *learn* how the body works, how to analyse skilled performances, how to prevent injury and how to organize and manage training sessions.

What do you need to know?

Begin with these three:

- Know yourself
- Know your performers
- Know your sport

Know yourself

Now is the time to stand back and ask yourself some searching questions.

How well do you know yourself?

It is vital to be able to assess yourself honestly and realistically. What are you like as a person? What are your strengths and weaknesses? Would your family and friends see them differently?

Remember that every individual is unique—performers *and* coaches. Do you understand how your own moods can affect your performers? You may know what stress does to them, but what does it do to you? Do you become anxious, over-excited and nervous during competition? If so, perhaps you need to learn some of the relaxation techniques your performers use! Your moods will probably be reflected by your performers, and hopefully in time they will learn to care for you as much as you care for them. You must be aware that your reactions will be different from those of your performers—make sure that you do not have a detrimental effect on them.

Never be too proud to ask for help—only a fool thinks he knows it all. Try to meet other coaches regularly to discuss training methods and to hear about new developments. Others may have found solutions to problems you are facing ... and you may have answers to their problems. This doesn't just apply within your own sport: get together with people from other sports too—they may have something important to pass on to you.

"The day you stop learning as a coach, you're finished." Knowing what you *don't* know is as important as knowing what you do! You will be expected to wear many different hats. Be honest—you can't be an expert in everything. Seek out those who have the knowledge you need, and learn from them.

You should sit down and assess your own strengths and weaknesses. Just like your performers, you should pay special attention to those areas in need of improvement—especially the things you like doing least. Don't take the easy way out by avoiding the difficulties—you would not expect that from your performers, so you should not accept it from yourself, either.

Don't be afraid to ask yourself just how good you are as a coach, and by what yardstick you measure your progress. Do you reckon your success by the number of medals your performers win, or by the help you are able to give them to develop on all levels?

Keep these questions in mind until Chapter 7, when we will look at them in more detail.

How committed are you?

You have almost certainly realized by now that good coaching requires total commitment on the part of the coach. You have to be responsible for seeing that *all* the factors necessary to achieve success are provided: your own time, your performers' time, the hire of facilities, the travel and accommodation, the equipment, the medical support—and *everything* else which may increase the performers' chance of success.

This means putting in a great deal of time—and, even more important, a lot of mental and emotional energy. Training and instruction is only a part of it: your commitment must extend to your relationship with your performers, counselling and advising them; and to thorough preparation for your coaching tasks.

This often puts a strain not only on you, the coach, but also on your family. It is essential that you and they come to an agreement as to how much of your time will be devoted to coaching. Otherwise resentment will build up, and serious domestic problems can result.

Task Make a timetable of your normal

week, listing the hours you spend at home, at work, travelling, coaching, at competitions, in leisure activities, and in other activities. Is the balance realistic? If not, make a list of the potential problems that might arise. How might you adjust the time-balance in order to overcome them?

Why did you enter coaching?

Every coach has his own personal motives for interest and participation in coaching. Be honest with yourself —examine your motives and try to state clearly to yourself why you coach and what you are gaining from coaching. There cannot be said to be "right" and "wrong" motives; rather, each person will find some different aspects of coaching stimulating and sustaining.

Task Make a list of what "turns you on" in coaching.

Know your performers

The problem with many coaches is that they think all their geese are swans! In other words, the coaches have world-shattering plans for their performers to make it to the top—but have failed to recognize that they have set out to win the Derby with the milk horse!

There are two aspects of knowing your performers: knowing *about* them; and knowing *them* as people. Both are important.

Knowing about them

Knowledge of the performer involves many factors. As a coach, you should have an idea of your performers' level of commitment. How much time, energy and effort are they prepared to put into their sport? What are their objectives? What do they wish to achieve? If the aims of the performer and the coach

differ, the chances of achieving a successful outcome are vastly diminished. In the case of young performers, what do you know about their home background and parental support? Don't forget, if the parents withdraw their support in either financial or moral terms, that probably means the end of the child's sports career.

Knowing them as individuals

You need to understand your performers as people so that you can help them make the most of their talent. This will help you to motivate them and help them cope with success and failure.

Competition may often be stressful, and performers can become anxious and apprehensive. You can learn to guide them sensibly through these periods of stress so that they can perform to the best of their ability. Understanding your performers' minds and emotions, as well as their bodies, is as important as understanding the techniques of your sport.

There will be many outside factors affecting your performers—home, family, friends, other athletes—and inside factors too—health, diet, emotions, moods, personal problems. People are complex, and there are no standard approaches that can be applied to all performers. For example, a bluff, hearty approach may be fine for some but disastrous for others. Spend time talking to each individual, getting to know him or her, before you work out your personal strategy.

We are not saying that you should only discuss personal matters, of course! Talk over training programmes and competitions on an individual basis, too. Draw up a "contract" (probably not a written one) between you and each of your performers, clearly indicating the expectations, commitment and goals that each of you has. Try to discover what your performers expect from you, and leave them in no doubt as to what you expect from them. *Goal setting* is an important part of your relationship. Work out the targets together—and be realistic: don't allow your hopes to overrule your common sense. It is good to have something to aim for, but if the goal is always out of reach your performer will fail and become discouraged, and your own credibility will suffer.

Mutual respect is important, and can only be established if you do not threaten one another's self-esteem. Do not chastise your performers publicly or shout at them after defeat. Learn to be firm but fair.

Some performers certainly require "geeing up" before a competition, but others will need calming down. Your instincts could well be right as to which is which—but they could equally be wrong! By applying simple tests you can determine which are the nervous performers and which are "laid back".

By setting a positive example yourself, you can help develop a positive relationship with your performers:

- Be enthusiastic
- Create a positive attitude towards training (and arrive punctually!)
- Ensure that every session has a purpose
- Give plenty of praise and encouragement

Task Give a brief "portrait" of any one of your performers in terms of objectives, commitment, parental support or social background. What problems does he/she have? Are you able to discuss these freely and offer help? How well do you really know this performer?

Recognizing talent

In many situations you will be in contact with young players or would-be performers, and can spot who is likely to be talented. However, you may not always be the one who recognizes potential talent. The newcomer may approach you on his own behalf, or come with friends; a youngster may be brought by a parent or sent by a teacher.

In whatever way they arrive, your job is to assess whether or not the potential athlete has a physical and psychological "profile" appropriate to the sport in which he wants to take part. By a profile we simply mean a set of relevant characteristics (such as height, weight and so on in the case of a physical profile) considered together.

Although top-class performers will usually have a correspondingly good profile, there are exceptions. Not all champions have "perfect profiles" by any means. So don't be too rigid in applying these criteria— especially not to young performers who have a lot of growing and changing to do.

Task Make a list of top performers in any sport who in theory should not have made it as champions. Why do you think they did?

One of the first things to find out is whether the potential athlete wants to undertake serious training with a view to competition. There is nothing wrong with fun-running and other kinds of recreational participation in sport; but you will want to put most of your time and effort into helping those who want to take it seriously.

Recruiting talent

The simplest way to find talented performers is to encourage as many people as possible to take part in sport and sport training. The more you look at, the greater your chance of spotting real talent. A good way of doing this is to have open sessions, or "taster" days as they have in rowing—making sure you advertise them as widely as you can in the local media.

Of course, one day's participation may not be enough for talent to show itself—often you need to encourage those who come forward to continue to take part for an extended period.

While talent-spotting is obviously important, you should not be elitist about it: the participants who don't show much talent will still benefit for the rest of their lives if you encourage positive attitudes to sport and health. It's a worthwhile exercise even if you don't find any potential champions!

In certain sports, such as gymnastics, potential athletes are positively screened by means of a series of tests for characteristics including range of movement, strength and coordination. This process can be effective provided the tests are well-designed, but in most sports it is not really necessary; simple screening by participation is sufficient.

Task How is talent-screening carried out in your sport? Could the system be improved? How?

Physical profiles

Performers who are to have the best chance of success in their chosen sport will need the appropriate physique and physical abilities. Olga Korbut at 16 was about 4 feet 10 inches tall and weighed less than 7 stone; there is no way that a 9-year-old girl who is already over 5 feet tall and over 8 stone is going to make it in gymnastics. Likewise, any would-be gymnast who cannot touch his toes

without bending his knees has little chance of success!

Other sports have their own criteria. Team games have the advantage of catering for many different physical types. Rugby caters for the fast and agile as well as the broad and heavy. In netball we find positional profiles: the tall players are generally either defenders or shooters, while the faster, agile, "springy" players are better suited to centre-court positions.

How can you find out about these profiles? Ideally, they should be deduced from rigorous scientific tests, and each sport should have its own profiles well documented. Unfortunately many sports have not yet reached this point in their investigations, and so finding out about physical profiles is not as easy as it might appear. However, if coaches examine the physical qualities required in their own sport, and analyse them, they can begin to build up their own provisional profiles. It will be interesting to see how far these are confirmed by sports scientists when full research has been done.

Task Draw up the ideal physical profile/profiles for success in your sport. Give examples of well-known performers with such profiles.

Psychological profiles

Many experts agree that it is the psychological side of sport which sorts out the champions from the rest.

Each sport will require different psychological abilities for success. The archer or marksman, for example, needs a different kind of personality from the prop forward or the sprinter.

However, there are certain common factors. In the early stages of sport training the coach should look for traits such as:

- love of the sport, shown by enthusiasm or joy in training
- determination
- competitive spirit
- the ability to concentrate
- intelligence (we mean "sport intelligence", as it might be called, not IQ or so many O-levels)

You should be aware that those who are keen, enthusiastic and full of love for the sport do not always make the best competitors. It is a *combination* of factors that you are looking for.

As with physical profiles, drawing up psychological profiles is largely a "do-it-yourself" process in most sports at present.

Task List the psychological attributes you think are necessary to achieve success in your sport. Do your most successful performers show these traits?

Know your sport

There is no substitute for knowing the techniques, rules and structure of the sport you coach.

Techniques need to be taught in the proper sequence and at the appropriate level. Techniques only become *skills* when they are used at the correct time and in the correct place (see Chapter 3). You have to be able to analyse techniques and teach your performers to apply them skilfully.

The coaching awards offered by most governing bodies of sport include all the relevant technical information, and regular courses are run throughout the year.

A complete and thorough understanding of the *rules* of your sport will help you to coach in a more meaningful way. You must work to make sure that your players understand and abide by the rules. The rules are there to ensure fair play for all, so learn them well and help your performers to use them to their best advantage.

It is important to understand the *structure* of your sport—how it is governed, and how decisions are made, by whom, and when. You are often on the receiving end of decisions, but if you understand what led up to them, both you and your performers will develop better.

What qualities do you need?

As Rod Thorpe says at the beginning of his Introductory Study Pack *Planning and Practice*, "You should recognize that there are different ways of coaching effectively—you may be a 'live wire' or the quiet but firm organizer!" Whichever you are, remember that groups will react to the enthusiasm you bring to the session rather than to the "loudness" of your approach. Chapter 7 gives more information about coaching styles.

Whatever your approach, there are certain things which will give you a good foundation on which to build.

Basic practical coaching knowledge

You must try to master the science, as well as the art, of coaching as it relates to performance. This means more than simply knowing the rules, skills and strategies of your game or activity. You have to try to:

- understand the human body, and how it responds to exercise
- understand the workings of the mind, and how it may be affected by stress
- analyse performance and monitor progress
- evaluate training programmes

- appreciate the nutritional needs of your performers
- understand the types of injury that may occur, and how you can play your part in rehabilitating your performers

Planning and organization

The ability to plan a meaningful programme for your performers is vital to your success. This involves planning each individual practice, each training session, each season and each year. Most of the great coaches in the world today have carefully organized programmes of training and competition that leave little to chance. Without thorough planning your performers will be held back from realizing their full potential.

You must try to prepare your work systematically, taking into account all the factors that will affect performance. If you plan well and create the right sort of environment, your performers will flourish. Keep records of what you do, how well it works (or doesn't work!) and the progress you make.

"Almost without exception, coaching literature ... stresses one specific point—that to gain respect a coach must be organized." Thus wrote R. Alderman in his 1976 publication *Basic sets of behaviour underlying successful coaching in sports coaching.*

Therefore build your plan carefully: think of it as a skeleton, a framework into which your performers' efforts can be fitted. It must be rigid enough to keep discipline in their training and coaching regimes, yet sufficiently adaptable to accommodate the changes dictated by the many factors which athletes have to cope with in the real world: factors such as time, money, facilities, competition, climate, attitudes and beliefs.

Performers enjoy activity, but "organized chaos" will soon result in boredom and disillusionment. Well-structured programmes help to build confidence and give the performer a feeling of achievement.

Relationships with others

A successful coach has to be willing to work hard at his/her relationships with others—performers, parents, administrators, officials, teachers and even spectators.

Performers

The relationship with the *performer* has to be based on mutual respect and understanding. The caring coach is usually the successful coach. Sensitivity in dealing with each individual is required, as not everyone responds to the same kind of approach (see page 76). Some coaches and performers simply cannot get along—not because the coach is bad or the performer awkward, but just because their personalities are incompatible.

Parents

In the case of a young performer, the relationship with his/her parents may be an important factor. As was remarked in the Introductory Study Pack *Safety and Injury*, "Parents come on a continuum from the demanding to the protective, and in some cases the over-protective! Parents' support is vital for young athletes, but good understanding and communication between parents and coach is essential for this support to be helpful rather than negative. There must be mutual understanding and acceptance of the roles of parent and coach, and clear lines of demarcation established." Talk to your performers' parents, find out what kind of pressures they may be applying to their children, and try to agree on what is best for the performer. Do not confuse the performer by giving conflicting advice— that will only result in unhappiness for everyone!

Administrators and officials

Sporting activities take place within a structured framework. Everyone has an important part to play. You need to develop an understanding of the rules and structures that govern your sport, and come to terms with what this means for you. You will always hear about the umpire/referee who "lost us the game", or the administrator who "does nothing but sit in committee meetings"! What must not be forgotten is that there are thousands of people in the "back rooms" of sport, all stoking the boilers. Some do it better than others; but then some coaches coach better than others, and some performers perform better than others. We are all human! Mutual respect can lead to closer co-operation and support.

As a coach you are a practical person working at the "sharp end" of sport, and no doubt you focus most of your attention on your performers. You probably have little time to attend committee meetings, debate policies, or devise development schemes for your sport. All the same, does your sport's structure embrace your performers' needs and aspirations? As a coach, you are in an excellent position to act as a link between the participants and the providers—take advantage of it!

Teachers

Many physical-education teachers are qualified coaches as well, and therefore wear two hats. But when the teacher and the coach are two different people, it is important that their efforts are coordinated to some extent. Often coaches do not feel that their sessions relate to the PE programmes being taught in schools. The teacher and the coach will probably have much the same body of knowledge to pass on to their performers, but may have distinctly different philosophies and objectives. Because of this, children can be given contradictory guidance. At best this results in confusion: at worst it may cause some to drop out of sport altogether. The demands placed on good young performers to compete for school and club can become an intolerable burden both physically and emotionally. This is why the coach and teacher need to talk in order to gain respect for each other's work and to provide the performers with a wide range of complementary experiences.

Spectators

The coach is often the target of abuse or adulation—he or she is the hero or the villain! It is not your job to court the crowd and try to win them over—they will always know better than you anyway! But try to set them an example: show them the right behaviour even after defeat or under pressure. You cannot control their response, but you can control yours.

Skilful communication

All the knowledge and planning will be of little use if the coach cannot communicate what he knows to his performers.

"No matter how much knowledge a coach has, no matter how great his understanding of the physical and emotional needs of his athletes, his success or failure ... boil down to one thing: communication. In his relationship with his athletes almost all of the coach's time will be spent in transferring his knowledge to those athletes and making sure they know what is expected of them." [T. A. Tutko and J. W. Richards, *Psychology of coaching*, 1971]

Communication is a skill that can be learned like any other. There are certain important techniques that you must acquire. Armed with these, you will develop into a skilful communicator as you learn to use the techniques appropriately.

What is communication?

So that you can succeed in presenting your material, it is important for you to understand the processes involved in communicating.

Communication can be defined as *the interchange of ideas and information by means of speech, writing or other media*. It is not just the transmission of information, but the interchange of ideas—a two-way process. Communication involves interaction between individuals or groups, and as such a whole range of social and psychological factors are involved. At the most basic level you need a common language: even differences of dialect or vocabulary can set up a communication barrier. Such things as different attitudes, feelings, drives, emotions and values can be equally significant.

Other external factors, such as what and how you communicate, are based on the specific situation. Peer groups, group norms and your expectations of the performers all affect the process of communication. To operate effectively as a coach you must be aware of these issues. Strive to establish a rapport, so that your listeners gain a real understanding of the meaning of what you are saying. Share your experience with them: true understanding is only possible from a background of shared experience.

Effective communication involves you in much more than just knowing the techniques of your sport. Some research studies have shown that as much as 70 per cent of your time as a coach is spent communicating, though this will obviously vary from one coach to another.

There are several key points that should help you to make your communication more effective.

- Reduce any "status awareness" between you and the group. It is all too easy to hide behind status, but this is a great hindrance to communication.
- Use language that is appropriate to the group. Avoid jargon that they won't understand.
- Use as many channels of communication as possible. A range of different ways of putting the information across is one of the hallmarks of a good coach.
- Try to eliminate any sources of interference, disruption or distraction.
- Face-to-face communication is usually best, as it allows for dialogue.
- As coach, you must accept responsibility for the effectiveness of the communication.
- Listen to what your performers say in response—then you will know how to say it better next time.
- Be aware of subliminal messages. If you have presented the same material several times before, for example, you may well look and sound bored. Make no mistake—this will come over to your audience!

Gaining attention

Communication is not just a matter of talking—or shouting! A whole range of *signals*—both verbal and non-verbal—are used to gain attention and to convey information or instructions.

Verbal signals

You have probably come across a coach who speaks softly yet loud enough to be heard. This technique encourages people to pay attention and to listen to what is being said. It also has the advantage of allowing for a louder volume when really necessary! Whereas if you shout all the time, noise levels in the group will rise to such an extent that verbal communication becomes well-nigh impossible.

Generally speaking, never stop the group until you know what you are going to say, ensuring that you are in a position from which you can coach effectively. In a gymnasium this is often with your back to the wall; on the water it might be alongside a crew; or out in the games field it might be in the appropriate quarter (rarely in the middle). A sound basic rule is to bring the participants towards you and to talk so that the performer farthest away from you can just hear you. Often you can check whether your voice is at the right volume by asking questions to see if they have heard and understood. A more experienced coach may use a more relaxed, spontaneous approach, but usually that is with a group where relationships have been firmly established.

As well as varying the volume of your voice, you can also vary your speed, inflexion or vocabulary. By these means you can either spur them into action or calm them down, softening the atmosphere. The voice is a very powerful tool for altering the emotions of the listeners. Coaches often have their pet phrases that act as a signal to the group for instant action or more effort.

Task Listen to the way a more experienced coach uses such phrases. Do you have any of your own? Do they have the desired effect?

If you intend to give a lengthy explanation (anything over a minute or so) it is probably best to bring the group in, ensuring that you can see all of them. Eye contact can help to present the information in a more meaningful and purposeful way. If you are working with children, it can be especially helpful to ask them to sit down, and to make sure they are not playing with small items of equipment while you are talking —though if they are, it may be a sign that you have gone on too long or have been talking above their heads.

Non-verbal signals

Eye contact has already been mentioned. Remember that "body language" communicates as effectively as speech. If you are slouched and looking at the floor, you cannot communicate enthusiasm no matter how arousing your *words* might be.

Many other techniques are available to you to gain attention without using your voice. These may include a whistle, horn or drum beat, or simply a raised hand. For these signals to be useful, the group has to be taught what they are expected to do when the attention signal is given. In the swimming pool, for example, a blast on the whistle may mean: "Stop - pay attention and listen for instructions". Experienced coaches will have developed the use of such non-verbal signals to such an extent that just a series of gestures makes the performers stop what they are doing, come round, sit down and await instructions, all without a word being spoken. The signals have become a matter of routine for them. This can be a valuable means

of saving time for the really important activities.

With younger groups you may be able to devise techniques to motivate them, such as turning the chore of putting the equipment away into a game by timing it against the clock.

The more expert you become as a coach, the more you will feel able to develop non-verbal ways of communicating with your performers alongside normal verbal communication.

Giving instructions

When giving instructions, gather the group close enough to see and hear you. Face them away from the sun and other distractions, so that their attention is focussed on what you are about to say.

When you wish to introduce the group to a new activity, a good way is to have a small sub-group (or just one individual) practising the activity in preparation for giving a demonstration, while the rest are still working on the previous activity. When you are sure that the new activity is working well, you can stop the others and show the demonstration. This makes the transition from one activity to the next very smooth.

If appropriate, make sure that the new technique is viewed from various positions: some techniques can look very different from a changed perspective. Check that your group understands what is required before sending them back to practise.

Instructions should be given in a clear, precise manner. You should always tell the group where to move, the signal to do so, and what to do then. Sometimes you can use other techniques for giving instructions, such as posting them up on the notice board, or using a blackboard. In some sports this way of presenting material is quite common, and it can be an effective way of scheduling a training session.

There are quite a few pitfalls to avoid when giving instructions:

- Don't use words that your performers won't understand.
- Don't repeat the same things over and over again in the hope that eventually they will get the message. Far better to think through what you intend to say and how to say it before speaking. A few brief, relevant statements can be very effective—especially on a cold day!
- Don't use redundant phrases such as "you know", "like" and "OK".
- Don't rush ahead without waiting until the whole group is listening.

The best way to avoid these pitfalls is to plan your instruction carefully.

Task From time to time, evaluate your own ability to give instructions. You can do this by tape-recording a training session and analysing it, bearing the above points in mind.

Presenting the technical model

When presenting a new technique to your group, it is helpful to give them the "technical model"—that is, a correct example of the technique in action. This can be done in many ways, visually, verbally or in writing.

When teaching physical activities and skills, the emphasis is usually placed on a visual model—a live demonstration of the technique which is easy for beginners to follow. If you cannot do this yourself, get an experienced performer to take your place. This method has the advantage that you can direct the group's attention to the most important aspects of the demonstration. Select two or three key points that you can explain to them

Chapter 3
How People Learn Skills

Careful study and experiment have produced certain *principles of learning* that provide a reasonable set of guidelines for coaches as they choose their teaching methods and techniques, and as they plan situations within which their performers can learn by experience. They include the following areas, developed in more detail below:

● Skills and techniques
● Motivation and rewards
● Recognizing individual differences
● Memory, learning and performance changes
● Learning-skills

Although these principles have an academic basis, they correspond with common sense. You should apply your own common sense to every learning situation. As your experience grows, you will become more skilled at selecting the best method for each situation.

What is skill?

We have already used the words "skill" and "technique" many times in this book—five times just in the paragraph above! They are often misused and misunderstood—and the worst confusion is caused by mixing them up. A skill is *not* the same thing as a technique. In essence, skill is the ability to *use* one or more techniques appropriately—at the right time, and in the right situation. Skill implies being in control of the situation, selecting your techniques, and combining them as necessary to do the job.

Be quite clear that it is wrong to confuse the task or the technique with the skill. You should be precise about how you use the term skill. After all, it is central to understanding what you—the coach—are about.

You should use the term "skill" when talking about a person's ability to be in control. Judge the extent to which a person is skilful by observing that person's action in demanding situations. Avoid thinking of only the action, the situation or the task as the skill. Skilful behaviour implies the appropriate "tuning" of the mechanisms which control behaviour. The right processes are activated at the right times in the right sequences. Skilful performance is the observable end product of employing good psychological strategies.

Skill is the result of learning. We learn how to achieve effectiveness, consistency and efficiency—the three most applicable descriptions of skilful performance.

Developing interest

Any skill, whether climbing, throwing, moneymaking or teamaking, will be acquired more easily and effectively if the novice has a motive for learning it. His attitude towards learning the skill will determine how much he learns and how well he learns.

So you must foster in your performers a desire to learn motor skills. They will learn if they are interested in what they are learning—if they experience immediate satisfaction; or see the need to build a strong, healthy body; or value the skill as something they can use in their leisure time. These are *intrinsic rewards*. Success in the activity is likewise effective at arousing and maintaining interest: this need not be competitive success, for acquiring a skill is in itself a form of success. You should encourage your performers to perceive skill acquisition in these terms.

It is also possible that learning can occur out of fear, or because of an extrinsic reward such as a star or credit given to the performer, but these motives are often less effective in stimulating learning.

The following guidelines follow from the above principles:

- Select activities that are appropriate to the group's interests, needs and capabilities. Can you think of examples in your own situation?
- Stress the intrinsic value of the activity.
- Present activities in such a way that each participant achieves some degree of success. How might you do this in your sport?

Individual differences

Performers are all different—they bring to each task their unique individuality. You will need to modify your approach to each performer, accepting and indeed encouraging the different ways in which they attempt to learn and eventually perform each skill.

The differences are due to both genetic and environmental factors, and the combination of these can provide startling contrasts between children, even if they are in the same age-group or class. The differences are often exaggerated when children are maturing physically, at puberty. Within a normal group there will be a range of about nine months in chronological (actual) age, but a mature 10-year-old may have a "maturational" age of 12—that is, he may be the size, weight etc of an average 12-year-old—whereas an immature 9-year-old may have a maturational age of 7. So the range of maturity in such a group may be as great as five years in development terms.

If children differ most markedly in terms of maturity, adults also differ in physical build, in psychological make-up and in their natural abilities. It cannot be assumed that an adult who is gifted in one activity will necessarily be gifted in another, even within the same game. Ideally, therefore, you will want to devise individual programmes of work for each novice. Usually this is not quite practicable, and you will arrive at a compromise, perhaps by introducing new work to the group as a whole, and then allowing for practice within small, fairly homogeneous groups. Further tuition and correction can be given within these smaller groups. From time to time, however, there must be opportunity for transfer between the groups, and for the stronger performers to practise with other, less skilful students. The stigma of failure must never be attached to the weaker groups, nor must the groups be allowed to develop into cliques, the more skilful forming an elite.

You must aim to be skilled at:

- organizing practices with groups
- organizing groups within a class
- assessing and recording the progress of individuals within each group (see Chapter 5).

Coaching children

Most coaches at some time in their careers have to deal with participants of all ages. Each age brings its own specific problems, both physical and mental. If the coach has responsibility for the safety, well-being and development of performers at the different stages in their lives, it is essential to know what they can reasonably undertake. Possibly the most critical stage in a sport career is in the early stages, i.e. the very young performer.

While obviously the personality and psychological capacities of the young are different from those of the relatively mature performer, there is as yet insufficient hard evidence to support theories concerning the psychological benefits and dangers of sport training and participation of young children. However, differences in emotional development are certainly important, affecting the children's stability, concentration and co-operation. Environmental influences may magnify these factors even more. There is a world of difference between the mature child with a supportive home background and the immature child who enjoys little encouragement at home. Team games are not merely exercises in physical skill, they are exercises in organization and co-operation. The immature child will find it difficult to co-operate, especially under the stress of competition.

If possible, you should try to match method to child in every learning situation, treating each child as an individual. Your aim must be to help each young person develop his or her full potential.

The physical effects of training are very much better known. The different systems of the body—for example the skeleton, heart/lungs, nerves—all develop at different rates. Factors such as height and weight tend to increase in phases or "spurts" rather than at a continuous rate, while other developments, such as the growth of the nervous system, are less easy to monitor. The important fact to remember is that children are *not mini-adults* and should not be treated as such. The stage they have reached in their development

dictates what they can be expected to achieve, and what it is safe for them to undertake. When planning the programme the coach should take all the relevant facts into account.

Early and late developers

We have already mentioned that children grow up at different rates. You must be wary of the pitfall of spending all your time on the early developer who is possibly athletically precocious. Beware! He may have reached his peak already and have little more to come. Conversely, don't neglect the late developer—he may surprise you!

Key guidelines

Children are to a large extent enthusiasts. Try to foster and develop that enthusiasm by remembering these key guidelines when planning your coaching.

- *Variety* Let children participate in as many activities as possible—don't restrict them unnecessarily.
- *Action* Children like doing, not listening, so allow as much active participation as possible (this is obviously not to the exclusion of all theoretical understanding).
- *Competition* Most children like to compete, and quite rightly, as that is one of the major components of sport. Always make sure they get some competitive activity even if it is only within the squad, team or group.
- *Enjoyment* Children, like most other human beings, will vote with their feet. If they don't enjoy your coaching they'll quickly leave the group.

Task Using the information obtained from other NCF books, make a list of

27

the different body systems. Next to them make a list of "dos and don'ts" of training at different stages of development.

Learning and performance

Whenever you do something you are learning: every activity involves using memory in some way. The recollection of how one did the same thing last time, acts as a guide for doing it this time. In this way a learned pattern of behaviour is built up. Memory is the means by which it develops, and there is a good deal of information available to you to help you decide which are the best ways to use your memory to develop skilful performance most effectively, efficiently and consistently.

You can safely consider the process of learning to be linked to changes in the internal structure of the central nervous system—the nerve pathways. These changes are relatively permanent and *accumulative*; that is to say, psychologists do not consider learning to have occurred unless changes in performance levels last for some time, or lead to new, more complex patterns of behaviour. Short-term changes in performance which are brought about by external influences and which do not persist when these influences disappear, are not classed as "learning".

What do *you* think learning is? The form your memory takes depends on the way you use it. If you practise widely differing variations on a technique you will easily be able to come up with the new movements demanded by changes in the conditions in which you perform. This requires a very general form of memory. If, on the other hand, you perform a very limited range of variations (perhaps just one way of doing something) then you will be able to

reproduce very closely similar movements over and over again. Specific repetitive practice leads to high reliability.

It is a useful "law" of human adaptation to training that effects will occur within the systems specifically *stressed*. (Think of the different kinds of physiological training and their consequent effects.) If you confuse skill with techniques, then in some sports (e.g. diving, swimming, gymnastics, rowing) you might be tempted always to organize practice sessions which emphasize very specific techniques with little or no variation. There is no doubt that performers will learn and adapt so that their memory can produce the appropriate strategy—given sufficient practice—but practising the same thing over and over again cannot be expected to have much effect on the performers' skill in learning.

The results suggest that transfer (see page 31) will occur to the extent to which the practice conditions *encourage* or *discourage* transfer. Psychologists consider that transfer gains are an indicator of how much memory is common to different tasks. These results suggest that the extent to which two "techniques" might be controlled by the same memory is purely a matter of how they are practised. Practise a technique in isolation, and it remains an isolated technique. Practise a technique in different contexts, and the knowledge gained is relevant to all possible contexts even those as yet unknown.

Skilful performance is the result of learning, but not all experiences necessarily lead to skilful performance. You will no doubt be able to think of many participants in your own sport who have acquired "bad habits". Of course, if you consider learning as a task then you can say that learners need to develop the skills of learning, just as you want to develop your skill in coaching. You can even go so far as to suggest that a skilful coach will encourage participants to develop as skilful learners, since skilful learners are less likely to waste time developing "bad habits" (and correcting them) and are, therefore, more likely to become skilful performers. They will learn effectively, efficiently and consistently—in a word, *skilfully*.

Such a view arises naturally out of an analysis of what all would-be skilful performers need. They need to be able to *get the most out of every performance* (whether in practice or competition) in order to *maximize the learning possibilities*. In this way they are always striving for better control and hence improved skill. In organizing training for skill you need to be aware of the effects your programme will have on the obvious performance skills that you can judge by watching. You must also consider the effects they have on the more fundamental skills which are essential for learning to occur. At this stage you need a list of such skills. Consider the following:

- Goal-setting—immediate performance goals/long-term aspirations
- Concentration and attention control
- Self-regulation—relaxation/activation
- Imagery—rehearsal/review
- Verbalization
- Use of feedback

Remember, to do is to learn, and what you learn is governed by what you do. So what your performers learn, whether they are novices or experts, will be governed by what you ask them to do. When you consider the ideas we have been looking at, you ought to be in a better position to understand why this is so. If you are now faced with a *new* coaching problem, you should be able to find a solution more skilfully.

Goal-setting

In your coaching you need consistently to emphasize the need for goal-setting. You must make sure that your performers always decide clearly what they intend to do. The goal must be appropriate in two senses:

First, the goal must be attainable. Setting an attainable goal is a skill in itself; the performer has to understand both the situation and his or her own level of ability.

Second, it must relate to aspects of the situation over which the performer can exercise control. A performer with the immediate goal of "winning" is not likely to perform well—he is more likely to do so if his immediate goal is related to the next specific task (a ball to be cleared to the right wing, or a vault to be executed with a better flight off the horse).

There is a great danger in setting too many *time* or *quantity* goals in skill training. Such goals as keeping going for five minutes or performing 50 repetitions are of obvious value, but if your performers are only used to setting such goals, they will not progress effectively when practice has to take other forms.

Appropriate goal-setting is perhaps the chief skill for learning, in that it sets up the system and prepares it for action.

Mental rehearsal

A number of techniques for mental rehearsal have been developed. There is strong evidence that mental rehearsal can be closely similar to the action being rehearsed, and that this is effective in improving performance.

In mental rehearsal, the mind will

organize the response but stop the body actually carrying it out. The memory responsible for informing the system about what to look for will also be linked in to the process. This cannot, however, be done if the performer has not yet developed enough knowledge and experience to allow him to predict what the outcome of the action should be. In other words, if the performer has not got a clear image, from his previous experience, of what the "ultimate" performance should be, he cannot reproduce it mentally.

Rehearsal is a powerful learning skill. Encourage performers to develop it.

Use of feedback

The benefits of mental rehearsal can be partly explained in terms of feedback. Another important sort of feedback is that which is given by a coach or any observer. There is an unnecessary distinction in the literature between two kinds of knowledge. *Knowledge of performance* is defined as information we give about the movement itself, while information we give about some measured outcome—for example, the accuracy of an attempt—is usually called *knowledge of results*. This is not a useful distinction, in that whenever you comment on a movement you will in fact have "measured" the performance against some standard that you consider to be the perfect or target performance. The key thing is that you will generally give feedback verbally.

The experimental data about what happens when we give such information seems to point to two apparently contradictory findings. First, the more precise the feedback, the better is the progress towards the desired goal (given that the performer understands the information given—always check this!). Conversely, we are not able to make *fine*

adjustments to control on the basis of verbal instructions. The mental levels responsible for handling verbal information and for carrying out precise instructions are too far apart. Let us illustrate this. We can demonstrate that virtually any adult can time a swing of a bat with an accuracy of ± 3 thousandths of a second (± 3 msec)! (Get someone to drop a tennis ball from a 6-metre-high balcony and hit it with the flat of your hand. The ball passes the hand in about 6 msec—if you hit it you must have timed your swipe very precisely.) A coach can get you to become consistent by timing the swing and giving feedback about the movement times. You will (after about 2,000 attempts) be able to perform so that each movement is never more than 5 or 10 msec away from the target "swipe" time. By this time you will probably not be taking much notice of the information about the times—the movement system will be "on automatic". The trouble will come if you are asked to take notice of a movement time, calculate the correction necessary and make it. If you are 6 msec slow you will go faster—but you will go much faster than necessary. After you have received verbal information which requires high-level processing, the accuracy of your conscious control is far less than that of the "automatic" lower-level system.

It seems clear that feedback in verbal form is very useful in getting behaviour *about right*. It therefore plays a very important guidance role earlier in learning, or when things have broken down over a number of attempts. Thinking about outcomes and working out what to do next is then of value.

Once you have a good idea of what goal-setting is all about, then thinking about *measured outcomes* is not as important as being aware of what is happening, rehearsing what to do, and reviewing what it felt like or what an observer saw. Passively focussing your attention on what you are actually doing is what is usually required. Information given by the coach then usually reinforces the learning process and reminds you of your goals.

Recent work has also shown that giving such information after *every* attempt does not necessarily produce the greatest learning effect. Bearing in mind the previous paragraphs, this should not surprise you too much. Collecting the information together in groups or blocks is perhaps a better way of talking to people about what they have done. Picking out an important aspect of performance, assessed over a number of attempts, is more likely to be of use than making comments on every trial. To assess performance in this way, you need to have a good grasp of match analysis: see Chapter 6.

If your comments are intended as *guidance* rather than feedback, drawing attention to the points during the practice, rather than after it, may be more useful. Performers often do not like this, yet paradoxically seem to benefit.

The exact timing of when to give information is also critical. While this may appear to contradict the previous paragraph, a good rule is to count to ten before starting to give feedback! A performer will need time to make sense of the information he has already got before getting any more. He may not even be consciously thinking about what happened, but the mind needs time to switch over from an "action mode" to an "understanding" mode.

Transfer

Transfer is the gains or losses in *performance* that occur as a result of the practice of a *different* task. Positive transfer means a performance gain brought about by doing something else, while negative transfer means a performance loss.

Task Write down an example of each from everyday experience and from sport.

Clearly, in performance terms, positive transfer would show itself by relatively permanent gains in performance of an unpractised task. Negative transfer would only be noticed if there were a relatively permanent deterioration in performance as a result of practising some other task. There is no experimental evidence to show that this occurs.

An alternative way of assessing transfer might be to look at how long or how much practice it takes to achieve some goal, a measure of the rate of progress. Positive transfer would then occur if practising one task leads to a better rate of progress on another task. Negative transfer in learning would happen if the rate of progress on the second task were slower following practice of another task, but fortunately evidence of this is slight. It seems that even if *initial* attempts are confused after practising something else, the amount of practice required on the *new* technique will not be significantly greater than if you were starting from scratch.

Task Appropriate goal-setting and rehearsal strategies should be firmly established for use in pre-event preparation. Can you explain why this should be so?

Chapter 4
Factors Affecting Performance

There are many psychological factors that can influence sports performance; some of these are shown in Figure 4.1. In this chapter we will focus mainly on three of these factors: stress, anxiety and self-confidence. The relationship between these and performance is unfortunately not simple, and at times it can be hard to understand. However, we have avoided the temptation to go in for simplistic and inaccurate accounts of the ways in which performers "blow it" on the day—these are worse than useless. After all, why should there be a simple account? Human beings are pretty sophisticated creatures!

Fig. 4.1 Some factors affecting performance

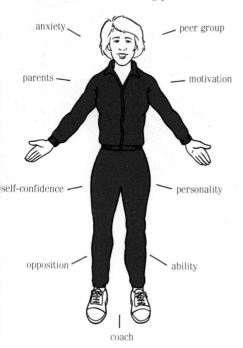

anxiety

peer group

parents

motivation

self-confidence

personality

opposition

ability

coach

Stress and anxiety

Definitions

Despite a colossal amount of research, psychologists working in this area still disagree on the definitions of the basic terms: stress, activation, anxiety and arousal. So it is worthwhile to explain first of all how these concepts are used here.

Stress can probably best be thought of as some sort of internal force meeting a resistance. For example, imagine a man leaning against the wall of a building. The wall will react by bending a microscopic amount and pushing back at the man; the two forces balance, and neither the man nor the wall are in danger of falling over. But if the man were replaced by an elephant the stresses would be much greater; up to a certain point the wall would still cope with the force exerted on it, but eventually cracks would appear and it would be likely to collapse.

In human terms, we can cope with low levels of stress because they cause us to become psychologically activated. A so-called *activation pattern* is set up which enables you to cope with the stress by "pushing back", as it were. However, too much stress feels threatening: near the limits of your activation range you will no longer feel stimulated, instead you are likely to become *anxious* and to start worrying about your ability to cope. The cracks are starting to appear, and already you are on the slippery road to self-defeat!

Arousal can be defined both psychologically and physiologically. At a psychological level, it is usually defined as the readiness of the organism to respond to a stimulus. This is effectively the same as activation level as described above. A highly aroused state is here described as an activation pattern, in order to distinguish it from physiological arousal as measured by heart rate, muscle tension, skin conductance and so on. These two notions of arousal are undoubtedly related, but probably not in any simple way.

Causes of anxiety

Research has shown that anxiety may be caused by four main types of situation:

- fear of physical harm
- ego threat
- fear of punishment
- fear of inanimate objects

Hopefully, the two latter causes of anxiety are not relevant to most sport situations, though gymnasts have occasionally been known to wince as they walk past their coach and the pommelled horse!

What all these causes of anxiety have in common is that, as you perceive the situation, your ability to cope is outstripped by the demands being made on you. It is not so much your *actual* ability to cope which is important, but how you *perceive* your ability to cope.

Symptoms of anxiety

When you know performers very well, it is often easy to tell whether or not they are anxious without even talking to them. Probably without realizing it, you are taking note of the symptoms of anxiety. These divide naturally into two categories, *cognitive anxiety* and *physiological arousal*. Some examples of each are shown in Figure 4.2.

Essentially, cognitive anxiety is anxiety you are aware of—actual worry or anxious feelings about the coming competition or whatever. Not all anxiety is of this kind: it is quite possible to be in a state of anxiety without consciously feeling anxious.

Physiological arousal is the body's natural way of preparing for "fight or flight". For example, the heart rate increases, to get more oxygen to the muscles where it will be needed; you sweat more, to moisten the skin and reduce the probability of its tearing, and also to disperse the extra heat generated by the faster metabolism; and you may feel a need to relieve yourself, thus reducing the excess weight carried and increasing speed (provided you're not caught with your trousers down!).

One well-established distinction

Fig. 4.2 Some of the symptoms of anxiety

- inhibition
- frightening images
- easily distracted
- worrying thoughts
- dry mouth
- lethargy
- nausea
- increased heart rate
- sweaty hands
- desire to go to the toilet
- increased adrenaline levels

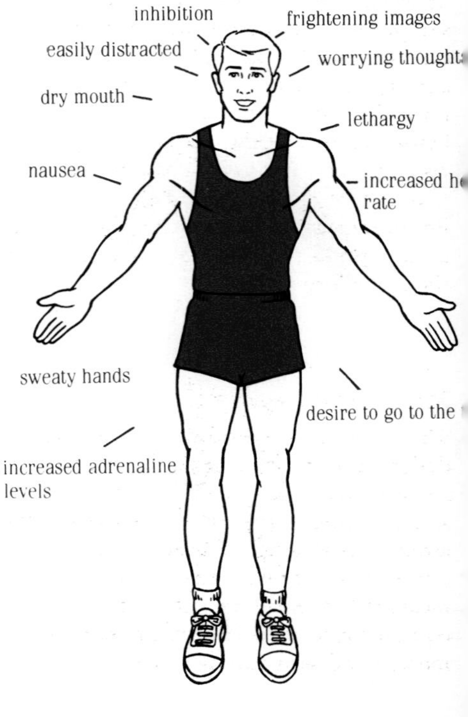

Fig. 4.3 Timing of cognitive anxiety and physiological arousal

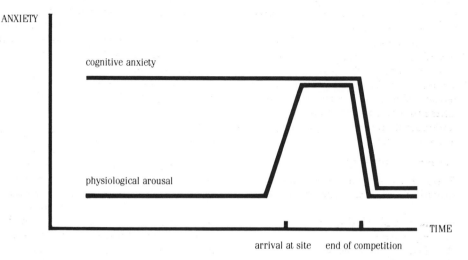

between these two kinds of anxiety symptom is that their timing is quite different (see Figure 4.3). Cognitive anxiety may be at a higher level than normal for up to two or three weeks before a major event, and generally remains fairly constant throughout this period before the competition. Physiological arousal, on the other hand, usually peaks late and fast, after arrival at the competition site.

Measuring anxiety

There are many questionnaires available designed to measure general anxiety levels in sportspeople. The better ones assess cognitive anxiety and physiological arousal separately. Of course, the physiological response can also be measured more directly by using equipment to measure heart rate, muscle tension and skin conductance.

Multidimensional arousal

Some older theories tried to explain changed behaviour simply in terms of the overall level of arousal. In doing so, they implicitly assumed that arousal and anxiety were one-dimensional and could be described by giving just one value, whether high or low. Today we regard both anxiety and arousal as multidimensional.

To explain this more clearly, imagine the activation system as an amplifier. If arousal were one-dimensional, we would be talking about a very simple, cheap amplifier with only one volume control to turn up or down. Multidimensional arousal is like a very expensive amplifier with lots of knobs to fine-tune the system exactly how you want it for the cassette or record you are going to listen to. It seems reasonable to assume that human beings, with our sophisticated and adaptable system, would possess an expensive rather than a cheap 'amplifier'!

35

A modern approach to the stress-performance relationship

Older research suggested that stress and performance were related by a curve shaped roughly like an upside-down U. This is no longer thought to be the case. A more realistic shape for the curve relating performance to stress is shown in Figure 4.4. This sort of curve is usually referred to as a catastrophe curve. It indicates that at low levels of stress performance should improve with increase in stress up to a certain critical point. At this point (point B in Figure 4.4) the performer starts to perceive that the demands of the situation are greater than his ability to meet them. Anxiety occurs, and performance suddenly and dramatically fails. After such failure the original level of performance can only be regained if stress levels are considerably reduced (to point A in Figure 4.4). This sort of phenomenon is very common in sport situations. Once a performer starts to "go over the top", it is very difficult to get him back up to a high level of performance.

Catastrophe curves like the one shown in Figure 4.4 usually occur as a result of opposing forces, and recent work suggests that this one is no exception. In competition these two forces are the desire to compete and succeed, and the fear of losing or failing.

Under normal circumstances the activation system "amplifier" is fine-tuned by the performer to meet the needs of his situation. However, when performers become anxious this fine-tuning is lost—in their anxiety they fiddle about with all the knobs, and so greatly distort their own performance. There is some debate as to how much effect the physiological response associated with anxiety has upon mental performance. However, there seems less doubt about its importance for physical performance, as any football coach who has witnessed the sustained speed at which a typical cup final is played will no doubt testify. Furthermore, it appears

Fig. 4.4 The stress/performance relationship which catastrophe theory predicts for experienced performers.

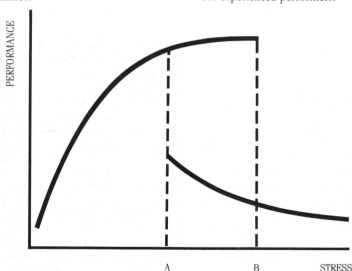

PERFORMANCE

A   B   STRESS

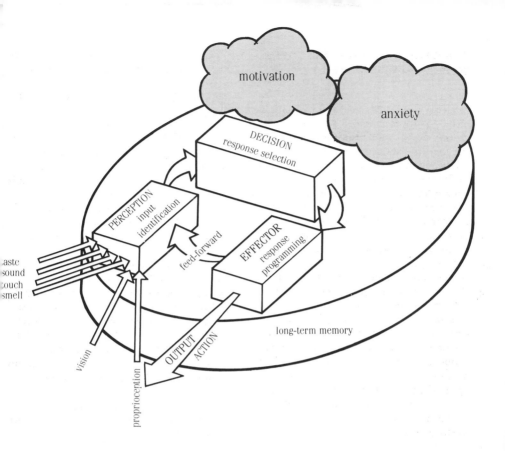

motivation

anxiety

DECISION
response selection

PERCEPTION
input
identification

EFFECTOR
response
programming

feed-forward

taste
sound
touch
smell

vision

proprioception

OUTPUT
ACTION

long-term memory

Fig. 4.5 Stressors and the activation pattern

that the distortion produced by excessive physiological arousal is most apparent in skills requiring fine control or touch.

The basic implication of the model shown in Figure 4.4 is therefore clear: to maintain performance in the face of anxiety you must either reduce anxiety or increase the "strength" of the activation system. To remind you of what we mean by the "activation system", Figure 4.5 shows how different "stressors" (factors causing stress) might affect the activation pattern of the information-processing system.

In order to perform difficult skills with accuracy and grace, the sportsperson must clearly "process" a vast quantity of information about the environment and his orientation within it. To do this, he must first of all perceive the relevant cues, then use them to make decisions about appropriate courses of action, "programme" these decisions into responses, and finally transmit these responses to the muscles. Of course, different situations will require each of these processes in varying degrees, so that the activation pattern necessary to achieve the best performance will vary from sport to sport, and from skill to skill within a sport. For example, speed of perception will be very important when close marking at basketball, but much less so when performing a set shot. In fact, the model shown in Figure 4.5 is itself an over-simplification, since each of the three major cognitive processes which we have distinguished—perception, decision-making and action—is itself made up of a number of sub-processes. For example, decision-making requires information to be *stored* in memory, *transformed* into likely consequences, and *recalled*—all before the information is passed on for programming. However, the model is sufficiently realistic for our purposes.

The important feature of the model shown in Figure 4.5 is that it represents the availability of each process by its elevation above the base plane. Fortunately, our brains are very flexible about how they allocate the resources at their disposal to each of these processes, so we are able to cope adequately with a great number of diverse situations. However, this flexibility is also our greatest weakness, for it means that the activation pattern required for a given situation can also be easily distorted by outside influences such as pressure from parents or coach, and also by internal influences like personality factors, anxiety and other negative mood states. The research literature suggests that the cognitive anxiety which is present for some time before an important event disrupts these activation patterns by:

● reducing the overall capacity of the system—pushing all the "process towers" down
● depressing the availability of some processes more than others.

On the other hand, it suggests that the physiological arousal that occurs immediately before performance tends to "turn up the volume controls" on all the output signals to the muscles. Thus errors which are due to problems in picking up the right cues or in making decisions about those cues are likely to occur several days before a big event, whereas errors due to output failures are much more likely to happen on the day.

As we mentioned earlier, the remedy for such distortion is either to build some sort of mental barrier to protect the processes by blocking anxiety, or to strengthen the resilience of the required activation pattern to such an extent that it cannot be easily distorted by anxiety. A coach and his methods of training can greatly influence this latter remedy, and at least partially influence the former. We look in more detail at how to overcome stress and anxiety problems in the next chapter.

Picking up the right cues

In many situations our visual perception system can be compared to a beam of light. You can have a broad focus when you want to attend to a fairly large area, or you can have a very narrow focus concentrated on a small area when you want to pick out fine detail. Of course, you can also vary the amount of movement of the beam about your field of vision. These two aspects of visual perception are called *narrowing* and *scanning* respectively. Under mild stress focus narrows, while scanning remains fairly stable. Under greater stress, producing anxiety, both focal narrowing and increased scanning occur. Focal narrowing, or "tunnel vision", can make it harder for the performer to observe team mates in better positions, for example.

Related to these concepts of focus is *selectivity* in perception. By this we mean the performer's ability to attend only to the things around him that are important. This apparently useful mechanism can also have disastrous consequences in sport. For example, footballers are quite likely to perceive the ball as the only important aspect of the environment, thereby ignoring all other sources of information. Football coaches usually refer to this as "ball watching". Cricketers likewise may be unable to use early cues from the bowler's hand and body position to determine the type of ball about to be delivered. This perceptual problem usually shows itself in hurried stroke production.

The combination of narrow focus, high selectivity and high speed of scanning has the effect of making anxious performers very easily distracted. Typically, for example, they will scan their field of vision very quickly with a very narrow focus in a desperate search for some "straw to cling to"—their coach, a friend, one of their own players, and so on. But the performer's problems are his own, and attending to distractions in this way merely clogs the system up with useless information.

When performers are anxious, their speed of *encoding* is also slower; that is to say, it takes them longer to perceive and understand the meaning of the important features of the situation. The ability to do this quickly is crucial in any sports environment which is subject to change; for example, deciding what sort of ball you are about receive when batting in cricket. This perception almost always occurs at a subconscious level, but it still has to take place before appropriate decisions regarding responses can be made.

Making decisions

Decision-making is probably the most widely affected of the cognitive processes shown in Figure 4.5. After all, some narrowing of focus and selectivity may

be quite a good thing, since it excludes irrelevant cues from the performer's consideration. However, decision-making is much more likely to be impaired by anxiety.

When the knowledge sources for a particular situation have been identified and encoded, the performer has to make decisions about exactly what to do in the circumstances under consideration. For example, a tennis player must decide which of the alternative shots to play, a hockey player whether to pass or dribble, etc. In complex decisions, cognitive anxiety slows down this process, while at the same time speeding up the throughput of information in very easy decisions. What we are saying here is that the effect of cognitive anxiety on the ability to make decisions depends on the number of factors which have to be considered in making the decision. Very simple decisions, which are almost reflexes, will be speeded up, but more complex decisions are likely to take much longer than normal to make. For example, in a "big match" it is not unrealistic to expect a football goalkeeper to make better "reaction saves", but to arrive late and drop high crosses around the edge of his goal area.

A very good example of the overall effect of high stress (though admittedly not competition stress) on decision-making comes from the climbing world. A recent expedition report described how two very experienced Himalayan mountaineers arrived at a safe place for a bivouac, and had to decide exactly where to cut a ledge out of the snow. They did not argue about it at all, but they still took a full two hours to arrive at a decision!

Information storage and recall

Under high anxiety, both the storage and early recall of information are also likely to be severely impaired. "Early recall" usually refers to the recall of information within two hours or so of its being stored. In a sports context this is the sort of time interval over which the performer must hold information about his opponent's strengths and weaknesses. Coaches and senior players in team games can, of course, help less experienced or more anxious players by issuing reminders about their opponents from time to time during the game.

In some sports (for example, ice-dancing, gymnastics and trampolining), performers are not generally required to make a lot of decisions during their performance. Instead they have to recall from long-term memory highly complex movement sequences. Research on long-term recall suggests that the long-term recall of what are called "low-association items" is impaired by anxiety, but that the long-term recall of high-association items may actually be improved. Low-association items are responses which are not well learned, while high-association items are responses which are so well learned that they are "automatically" invoked by the appropriate stimuli.

One implication of this finding is that in highly stressful situations, such as the last round of a very tight gymnastics competition, it is probably a good idea to use "old, fairly safe" techniques rather than newly-acquired and worrying ones. This may require performers to be quite flexible in their approach, and even to set multiple goals.

In some sports this effect can also work the other way round, as performers who are attempting to play very safe are likely to revert to stereotyped moves when under high stress. For example, a judoka may rely on his few "favourite" throws, despite having spent a vast amount of time in training learning a new throw specifically for this particular

fight. It's the phenomenon of "they can do it in training, but they can't do it in the game"!

Getting to grips with the problem

In mild cases of competitive anxiety, it should be possible to reduce the disruptions to the activation system by encouraging your performers to adopt specific strategies. For example, a rugby winger who is poor at anticipating changes in direction when tackling might be encouraged to look at his opponents' hips for cues; or a squash player who has difficulty memorizing an opponent's weaknesses during a game might be given a short mental checklist to work through during the "knock-up" and the first few rallies.

However, in more serious cases these strategies are unlikely to work. We shall look first at certain anxiety-blocking strategies, and then at ways of stopping these problems from occuring in the first place.

Anxiety-blocking strategies

Most anxiety-blocking strategies make use of relaxation techniques. There are a large number of these techniques, and they can usually be categorized according to their physical, cognitive (mental) or behavioural emphasis.

For example, *progressive muscular relaxation* is an essentially physical technique by which you can learn to relax each muscle group in your body, either individually or all together.

Conversely, *standardized clinical meditation* is a psychological technique which enables you to focus your attention inwards while blocking "negative thoughts".

Finally, *behaviour therapies* usually require you gradually to approach a eared situation while maintaining physiological arousal at a low level.

The exact technique prescribed for a given problem is usually determined by a number of factors, including both the source and the symptoms of the anxiety. For example, a gymnast suffering from excessive muscle tension at competitions (forced swings, fast double leg circles, loss of timing, etc.) might find a physical relaxation strategy like progressive muscular relaxation more helpful than a mental strategy like standardized clinical meditation. On the other hand, psychological strategies can be very useful for reducing negative self-talk and improving the self-confidence of a performer. While a detailed understanding of these sorts of techniques requires more psychological knowledge than most coaches at present possess, the ability to relax is an essential "life skill" which all performers and coaches should possess, and it is for this reason that we have mentioned these techniques here.

Self-confidence

Another important way for you to reduce your performers' long-term susceptibility to anxiety is to improve their self-confidence. Although as a coach you should have a concern for your performers' general self-confidence, here we are interested in your performers' self-confidence in specific situations—which is quite different and not necessarily related. For example, a tennis coach may want his tennis players to demonstrate great self-confidence in tennis matches, but need not be very interested in how self-confident his players are on a trampoline or while rock-climbing. This sort of situation-specific self-confidence is usually called *self-efficacy*.

Essentially, self-confidence is the performer's belief that he has the ability to succeed and that his activation system is correctly set up, with all the processes that he will need in order to succeed being available to him. In a sense, then, self-confidence represents the force in the catastrophe curve (Figure 4.4) which is to do with the desire to compete and succeed, while anxiety represents the force to do with fear of losing and failure.

Notice that it is possible for an expert to be both anxious and self-confident at the same time; that is to say, he may worry about the consequences of the forthcoming event, but still believe that his activation system is correctly set up and hence that he can win.

Goal-setting

An American psychologist called Bandura has shown that confident performers are higher achievers, and also more persistent in the face of failure. He has suggested that a performer's self-confidence can be influenced by four main factors:

1 previous success (performance accomplishment)

2 observing others succeed (vicarious experience)

3 verbal persuasion (you can do it!)

4 positive (or negative) interpretation of physiological arousal

Of course, all these factors are important determinants of self-confidence, but the crucial thing about Bandura's work is that it implies that performance accomplishment is by far and away the most important of them. As we have just indicated, performance accomplishment is about success, and success is about achieving goals. The more goals achieved, the more success the performer experiences, and the greater his self-confidence becomes. Moreover, he will be more persistent in his attempts to cope with similar situations.

The relevance of all this to the coach should be clear: as we saw in Chapter 3, *the setting of appropriate goals is critical for all performers in all sports.*

Structured learning with task requirements gradually increasing in difficulty may assist goal-setting, but the position is far more subtle than this. Goals must be structured, but recent work has also shown that goals are much more effective if they are short-term, set specifically for the performer and the situation under consideration, lie totally within his control, and are accepted by him. For example, we would not consider a goal of becoming British champion appropriate for a national squad swimmer, because it lies largely outside his control. (It might well be a realistic long-term aim, but this is a different matter.) Specific goals within the control of the performer should:

- set a target for the next competition
- reduce the influence of other performers upon that target to a minimum.

Consideration of these two factors leads to the view that effective goals must be set in terms of scores or times, rather than positions (e.g. coming first). Of course, this is much more difficult in team games where a score is also highly dependent on other people. However, with a little bit of ingenuity, and knowledge of the opposition, realistic and appropriate goals can still be set. For example, in a netball match a goal defence player might set herself the target of stopping the opposing goal attack from getting in more than two close-range shots during the game. With

this sort of goal the influence of other players is at least limited.

It is also worth emphasizing the importance of goal acceptance. The setting of specific goals only improves performance if the goals are accepted by the performer as being attainable and worthwhile. Once again performers differ in the way they like to set goals: some will prefer you to take the lead in setting goals for them, while others will prefer to propose their own goals and then confirm them with you. Either way, if performers are to accept their goals, they *must in some way participate in setting them.* Goals should not be simply assigned by the coach.

How difficult should goals be?

A picture of the relationship between performance and goal difficulty clarifies some of these points (see Figure 4.6). For specific goals which are under the performer's own control, this relationship is such that as goal difficulty increases so too does performance, up to a certain point A; thereafter, performance decreases. The precise location of point A is determined by whether or not the goal is accepted by the performer. Thus, the relationship between performance and goal difficulty is positive provided the goal is accepted by the performer, but negative otherwise.

Published literature suggests that the critical point A lies around the 70 per cent difficulty level; that is to say, goals which are only 30 per cent achievable (more likely to fail than succeed) should produce the best level of performance. However, this literature is largely concerned with fairly unmotivated subjects performing mundane industrial tasks, and experience in sport is somewhat different. The literature also generally fails to consider the effect of

Fig. 4.6 The relationship between goal difficulty and performance

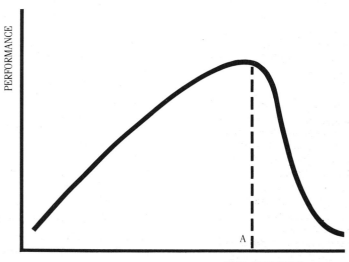

performance anxiety upon the relationship between performance and goal difficulty. However, the evidence that does exist on the relationship between anxiety and goal-setting suggests that anxiety reduces goal-acceptance, possibly by as much as 30 per cent (see Figure 4.7). Thus, as competition approaches, anxiety increases and doubts begin to occur about the balance between the demands of the situation and the performer's ability to meet them. Gradually, a goal which seems perfectly acceptable when it is set during training may well begin to look far too high and totally unacceptable for the stress of competition. The performer and his coach must therefore lower their goals for competitions, particularly where anxious performers are taking part in major events.

The following anecdote illustrates this point well. A coach was working with a semi-professional football team which had not won a single point for three months. Most of the players had started to cope with their pre-match anxieties by setting individual goals in consultation with the coach. However, on the last Saturday before Christmas the team faced the daunting task of playing the league leaders (who had not dropped a point) away from home. No one was relishing the prospect. After some soul-searching, the coach decided the best thing was to admit that the team was "on a hiding to nothing" and to lower the goals still further—and they were already pretty low! The transformation was miraculous. Given goals which they accepted as being within their reach, the team played magnificently in the first half, and were 2–1 up at half-time. But the crucial half was obviously to come. Throwing caution to the winds, the coach told the team they "still did not stand a cat in hell's chance" of winning, and that they must stick to their personal goals. After 20 minutes they were 3–2 down, but

43

they did indeed stick to their goals and came back to 3–3, eventually putting the opposing team under a lot of pressure. This match was a turning point. They continued to work at low personal goals throughout the season, and as it wore on they achieved modest but worthwhile success.

The exact amount by which goals should be reduced is the subject of current research. Most performers are unlikely to be positively motivated if they experience failure more often than success—that is, if their goals are less than 50 per cent achievable. Obviously, there are also large individual differences in the amount of self-confidence that performers possess, and so competition anxiety causes a correspondingly variable degree of reduction in goal-acceptance. As a rule of thumb in most sports, competition goals should be set at a level which the performer could expect to achieve at least 70 per cent of the time during normal training.

Factors which might increase the optimum level of goal-difficulty include high self-confidence, experience, and the simplicity of the task to be performed. For example, a young gymnast entering her first national competition should certainly be able to perform her voluntary routines at least 70 per cent of the time during training, while a confident and experienced marathon runner entering a major event might choose to set himself a goal which he has never before achieved.

Our 70 per cent achievability figure contrasts rather sharply with the sorts of level for goal difficulty that have been suggested by some other sport psychologists (e.g. Rushall, 1979). Nevertheless, we feel that ours is a more appropriate goal-difficulty level, particularly bearing in mind the moral

Fig. 4.7 How anxiety influences the relationship between goal difficulty and performance

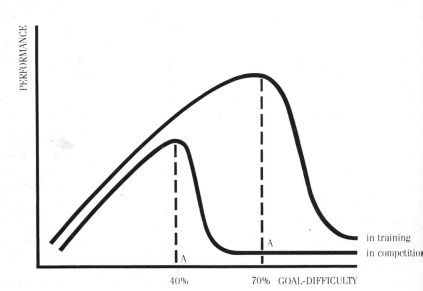

responsibility that all coaches have to help their performers achieve a feeling of self-worth. Encouraging a performer to set goals which are beyond his ability may well improve his *short-term* performance, but a performer who consistently fails to achieve the goals he aims for is likely to become first of all frustrated and then self-critical, despite the improvements in actual performance that may have occurred. This moral responsibility is, of course, even greater with young or disadvantaged performers.

Unfortunately, apparently easy goals are quite likely to create acceptance problems of a different nature for some performers who may feel that such low goals do not match their ambition. This sort of "high-achievement motivation" can be very useful in a performer, but it can also be disastrous—particularly if the performer is of an anxious disposition. The coach obviously needs to handle such a situation with great sensitivity and tact. On the one hand, he knows that he must lower his performer's goals, but on the other the performer must not feel that the coach has forced his own goals upon him. Explanation of the factors underlying goal setting may help, although ultimately the coach may have to resort to asking his performer to set goals during a mock competition when he is already under stress. This stress can be increased by introducing unknown audiences, biased judging, opponents and competitive noise, etc.

See Chapter 5, pages 52–53, for a detailed outline of how to set multiple goals for an entire season's play.

Seeing others succeed

The second of Bandura's factors, vicarious experience, is also an important one for coaches to know about. The literature which is available on this subject suggests that modelling (the traditional method of coaching with performers watching a demonstration before practising a skill) is much more effective in terms of improving self-confidence if the model (demonstrator) can be easily identified with. It follows that, with performers who are nervous or lacking in self-confidence, it is probably a good idea to use someone from the same group who can only just perform the skill, rather than an expert who performs the skill with ease. Perhaps this is a case of "If he can do it, so can I". However, this may well not be so useful for advanced performers training to perfect their technique. Such performers are much less likely to be lacking in self-confidence during the later stage of skill acquisition and will want to have access to as much technical information as possible about the skill. Notice that the phrase "have access to" does not imply that you should necessarily *say* anything.

Imagery can also be used as a form of vicarious experience. Imagery is a form of mental rehearsal in which you see yourself performing a skill. The pictures you see may be the same as you would see if you were actually performing the skill (internal imagery), or how someone else would see you if they were watching you perform the skill (external imagery). However, whichever of these you use there is some evidence to suggest that feeling, hearing and even smelling the situation will help improve the benefit of imagery. Although it is not yet clear exactly how imagery aids performance, it is thought that one way in which it works is by helping the performer to concentrate on the goal and set up an appropriate activation pattern to achieve it. Another may be by helping to locate appropriate sources of feedback.

A number of sports psychologists have used imagery in conjunction with

progressive muscular relaxation to increase self-confidence and reduce anxiety in top-class performers from a large number of sports. Richard Suinn has been one of the leading proponents of this technique, which in spite of its rather daunting name *visuo-motor behavioural rehearsal* is actually quite simple. First, you use progressive muscular relaxation for about 20 minutes, and then you imagine yourself successfully performing the problem skill. Using this technique, Suinn has been able to reduce anxiety in Olympic ski racers even on the day of the event. However, we would suggest that if you are to avoid alarming your performers you should practise the techniques of relaxation and imagery with them thoroughly in training first.

Talking them through it

Verbal persuasion, the third of Bandura's factors, is perhaps the most overworked by some coaches! The most important thing to realize about the effect of verbal persuasion on self-confidence and anxiety is that verbal persuasion and harassment are not the same. Shouting at anxious performers, telling them to concentrate on what they are doing, or even just indicating their mistakes, is only likely to make them more anxious if they are unable to do anything about it. Verbal persuasion is about encouraging them to accept goals that they can realistically expect to achieve.

Finally, altering the way in which performers *interpret* their physiological arousal state is generally beyond the scope of this book.

Overlearning

All the disruptions to performance listed above have one common factor: they are all reduced by *overlearning*. Overlearning is like this. If it takes you 200 attempts to learn how to do something, it will take you at least another 200 to be able to reproduce it reliably *when you are not under any competition stress*. To be able to reproduce the skill under high competition stress will clearly take a lot longer. Of course, overlearning implies lots of success, and therefore lots of self-confidence!

In the same way, the personal skills involved in goal-setting, imagery and verbal persuasion cannot be expected to function adequately if they are not practised thoroughly. They too must be acquired and overlearned if they are to be effective.

Chapter 5
Preparation for Competition

Many coaches believe that the only way a performer will learn to "handle" competition pressure is to get lots of experience in competitions. However, this neglects some potentially very powerful experiences which are readily available to performers. There are at least three areas of experience which performers can draw on in order to learn how to maintain, or even improve, their performance under external stress.

First, there is experience gained from actual competitions. It is generally held that this is the most valuable form of experience available. However, while it is undoubtedly true that one can learn much in this way (win or lose), such learning cannot occur without proper preparation beforehand and evaluation afterwards. This means that there must be enough time between competitions for the performers to plan and prepare themselves—especially in the case of youngsters who have still to learn how to do so. In reality, performers usually learn less than could be expected: successes are more usually attributed to "getting it all together", and failures to poor refereeing, bad lighting, "dirty" opponents, etc.

The second source of competition experience is from mock contests and structured training situations. These training situations can be used to introduce competition factors in a controlled way so that performers can gradually learn strategies to cope with them (see *Concentration training* below). To encourage self-confidence (see page 41), these learning experiences should be structured to produce positive outcomes as often as possible. If they do not, they

should be modified and repeated until they do.

The third source of experience is one's own imagination. As we have seen, mental rehearsal, or imagery, is much used by elite performers both in training and during competition. It is very effective when used alongside actual experience.

All three of these different forms of experience can be used to help performers improve control in their competitive environment.

General preparation

Clearly, great differences exist between sports in the amount of time that performers have to prepare for a given competitive event. Many top gymnasts compete in only a small handful of major competitions each year, while a First Division footballer is likely to play over 60 games in 7 months. However, exactly the same principles apply to competition preparation regardless of this. What may well vary is the proportion of the available time which is spent on general preparation for competition.

In this section we will discuss general strategies that can be used by performers in any competition.

Concentration training

In Chapter 4 we discussed in some detail the way in which competition anxiety may affect perception. Because such anxiety causes increased focal narrowing, scanning and selectivity in perception, anxious performers tend to be easily distracted by things which appear to be relevant, but in fact are not. What is needed is something to improve the performer's *concentration*.

One way to help your performers improve their concentration in the face of such distractions is to play "distraction" games. These are games in which one performer deliberately tries to distract the other(s) by any means he can, so long as he does not physically impede their movements. Obviously, such sessions must be carefully structured if they are to remain safe. Initially, there should be very strict rules about what the distracter is allowed to do, or alternatively you might restrict the performers to very simple tasks. However, with practice, your performers should gradually become capable of maintaining their concentration in the face of bigger and bigger distractions. As well as increasing general resistance to distraction, this technique can also be used to help improve your performers' concentration in the face of specific distracters such as bad refereeing decisions, niggling opponents, verbal abuse, etc. With a little bit of imagination you can structure any sort of environment you want, so that your performers can gradually become desensitized to the specific stimuli that they find off-putting. You just tell your distracter(s) what to do.

Suppose, for example, you want to help a basketball player who is easily distracted by bad refereeing decisions and who therefore tends to criticize other decisions and to make silly mistakes himself during the next few minutes after having been distracted. The answer is to arrange your training sessions so that bad decisions are deliberately given during certain practice games. You must explain what you are going to do, and how it will help, otherwise he may simply get frustrated and give up.

To begin with you should only give one or two bad decisions against the player, but gradually build the number up until he can handle however many might occur in an actual game. At times the player will cope well, but at others he will lose his temper, and will need to be reminded gently of the point of the exercise. Eventually, when he has learned to cope with these "declared distraction" games, you must introduce bad decisions into practice games without giving any warning beforehand, so that he learns not to be distracted by them even in a "real" game.

Competition training

This same idea of gradually desensitising your performers to harmful stimuli also forms the basis of *general competition training*. In this sort of training, an artificial competitive environment is constructed over a number of training sessions by gradually introducing more and more aspects of the true competitive environment. For example, a competition training programme for gymnasts might gradually introduce judging, formal warm-ups and waiting periods, co-performers, "bad" scores, audience noises (tape-recorded), and even a live audience. Provided that it is well constructed, this sort of competition training is generally very effective, particularly with performers from aesthetic sports in which performance is judged subjectively, such as Olympic gymnastics, modern rhythmic gymnastics, ice dancing, high-board diving, and kata in karate.

These mock competitions may still cause some performers to experience so much competition anxiety that they are unable to perform well. In such cases the use of the following general relaxation strategy may help.

Physical relaxation

Physical relaxation is not a panacea: it will not solve all of your performers' problems. However, it will help in some circumstances, and it is a necessary prerequisite for learning many of the more advanced skills.

Perhaps the simplest physical relaxation technique to learn is *progressive muscular relaxation* (PMR). This enables you to gain precise control of the levels of tension in each individual muscle group; so it is not just an anxiety-reduction technique, but also a direct aid to skilful performance: that is, it enables you to use only those muscles which you actually need to perform a technique, thereby producing efficient, effortless movements.

First you must find a comfortable position to sit or lie in, such as:

● sitting in an armchair
● lying flat on your back
● lying on your front in the recovery position

Most people find it easier to relax if they do the PMR exercises in a darkened room by themselves. It is also easier to reduce external distractions if you close your eyes. Do not worry about distracting thoughts; these are natural and will decrease with practice. Simply let the distraction pass, and re-focus on the task in hand.

The PMR session may be so successful in relaxing you that you fall asleep! Choose your time and place appropriately, therefore. A PMR session in bed before you go to sleep is obviously quite sensible, whereas it is not a good idea to do it before strenuous exercise.

Essentially PMR works like this: you divide the body into its major muscle groups, and work through each of these in turn, first tensing the muscles and then relaxing them, focussing your attention on the difference in sensation between tension and relaxation. The muscle groups are:

● the shins and calves
● the thighs and buttocks
● the small of the back and the stomach
● the chest
● the shoulders and arms
● the face and neck

With each exercise, you should sink gradually into a deeper and deeper state of relaxation. After working through each muscle group, you should continue to relax throughout your body while focussing your attention on relaxing still more deeply by breathing slowly and fully, using only your stomach muscles, and concentrating on sinking deeper with each exhalation. At the end of any relaxation session it is important not to jump up suddenly, but to wake yourself up gradually and gently, so that you feel calm and refreshed.

A word of warning is appropriate here about using general relaxation strategies to reduce anxiety in this way. If you think back to the analogy of the physiological arousal system being like a sophisticated amplifier, it should be clear that a general relaxation strategy has the effect of turning *all the knobs down*. Since the "anxiety gremlin" may have turned some knobs up more than others, this may not produce an optimal physiological or psychological state. However, because of the catastrophe curve of performance described on page 36, it seems likely that a performer will be able to regain that optimal state more easily from a position of general underarousal than from a position of general overarousal. Therefore successful mental rehearsal following relaxation, but before performance, may help to get the performer's activation state back to what it should be.

Of course, with all these strategies, you should first of all discuss the purpose and precise nature of such training programmes with your performers (and their parents) before embarking upon them. For, although there is nothing mysterious about any of the techniques, a "mystique" does unfortunately surround much of what has been written on psychological preparation for sport.

The skills and strategies which have been introduced in this section, together with those discussed in Chapters 3 and 4, form the foundations upon which the mental preparation of performers for specific competitions can be built.

The psychological importance of planning

In this section we will consider strategies which are aimed at enhancing performance for specific competitions. Perhaps the most important thing to realise here is that competitions do not usually occur in isolation. Most performers' long-term aims will require them to be "successful" across a whole season, or at least a large part of it. Chapter 4 outlined the importance of setting appropriate goals at all stages. Consequently, it is necessary right from the outset to plan weekly and monthly goals for training and competition in order to achieve these long-term aims. Your performers must be fully involved in this goal-setting process so that these long-term plans are self-motivated, not imposed by you. In the same way, you must discuss and clarify the means by which you and the performer will evaluate progress and performance.

Planning the season's goals

One way to plan a season's goals is as follows:

1 With your performer, write down three long-term but realistic aims for the season, bearing in mind the usual constraints that they must be within your performer's control, and must be open to quantitative assessment rather than mere subjective opinion.

2 Decide which of these three long-term aims is the most important and put a letter A next to it. Similarly, mark the next most important aim with a letter B, and the least important one with a C.

3 For the long-term aim A, determine and write down three goals which you will achieve in the next month to help you achieve A. Now put a number 1 next to the most important of these, a number 2 next to the second most important, and a number 3 next to the least important. Also determine one goal for the long-term aim B which you can achieve in the next month, and which will help you to achieve this long-term aim. Number this monthly goal 4. You need do nothing about long-term aim C as yet.

4 Now, for monthly goal 1, determine three immediate goals, or courses of action, which you will complete this week in an attempt to achieve this goal. Similarly, select two immediate goals, or courses of action, for monthly goal 2; but do nothing about monthly goal 3 for now. Finally, select one immediate goal, or course of action, for monthly goal 4.

You should now have six immediate goals, or courses of action, which you will attempt to complete during the coming week. Five of these immediate goals are aimed at achieving your monthly goals 1 and 2, which are in turn aimed at achieving primary long-term aim A. The sixth of your immediate goals is aimed at achieving your monthly goal 4 and, via this, long-term aim B. Notice that your immediate goals do not need to be performance-orientated. For example, a suitable immediate goal might be to arrive on time for training every day, to buy a new piece of equipment, or not to "give in" when training is going badly.

Figure 5.1 shows such a schedule of goals for an eighteen-year-old male gymnast, who had previously been a member of the British Junior Squad, but had just become too old to belong to that squad.

At the end of the week evaluate your success in terms of goal-achievement, re-evaluate your monthly aims, and set six new goals for the following week, using the same method as you used before. Similarly, at the end of the month evaluate your success over the month, re-evaluate your yearly aims, and set three new goals for the next month. Finally, do the same to evaluate the progress you make over the whole year.

Fig. 5.1 Multiple goal-setting for a male gymnast decided by the gymnast, together with his coach, following a discussion of the previous season's progress

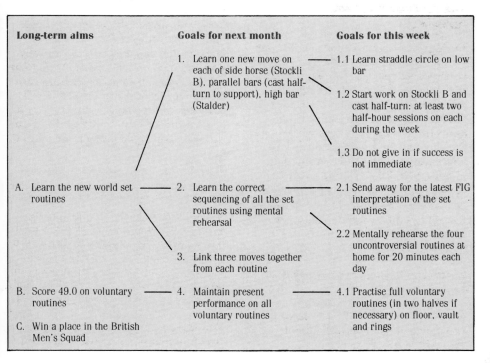

Long-term aims	Goals for next month	Goals for this week
	1. Learn one new move on each of side horse (Stockli B), parallel bars (cast half-turn to support), high bar (Stalder)	1.1 Learn straddle circle on low bar
		1.2 Start work on Stockli B and cast half-turn: at least two half-hour sessions on each during the week
		1.3 Do not give in if success is not immediate
A. Learn the new world set routines	2. Learn the correct sequencing of all the set routines using mental rehearsal	2.1 Send away for the latest FIG interpretation of the set routines
		2.2 Mentally rehearse the four uncontroversial routines at home for 20 minutes each day
	3. Link three moves together from each routine	
B. Score 49.0 on voluntary routines	4. Maintain present performance on all voluntary routines	4.1 Practise full voluntary routines (in two halves if necessary) on floor, vault and rings
C. Win a place in the British Men's Squad		

Assessing goal achievement in competition

Obviously, some sports lend themselves much more readily than others to objective goal-setting which is entirely within the performer's control. However, with a little bit of thought and some knowledge of the technical requirements of your sport, you should be able to assess many aspects of your performer's play objectively, even in team games. The key to this sort of assessment is to draw up a match-analysis sheet for each individual or functional group within your team. See Chapter 6 for full information on match analysis.

Clearly, the markers who assist in preparing analysis sheets or reports need to be trained how to score such sheets in order that each player is being judged according to the same scale. The easiest way to do this is probably to have the marker score a player alongside yourself or another experienced marker. Potential markers who fail to adopt a similar criterion to you within a few attempts should be rejected, as this sort of difference may well indicate that the person concerned works to a fundamentally different set of values to your own.

Another way to reduce this problem is to have each player scored by three independent judges and then take the average of their scores. There is a good deal of experimental evidence showing that this method of using panels for judging considerably increases its objectivity.

Skill development versus skill maintenance

Skill development is the art of producing new skills, or developing additional refinements to old ones. Skill maintenance, on the other hand, is the repetitive practice of previously learned skills to keep them up to scratch. This distinction between skill development and skill maintenance training is an important one. You might think that if the appropriate skills have been developed, maintenance of performance under pressure will automatically follow, this performance in turn leading to the further development of skill. Unfortunately, many performers do not possess the skills needed to maintain performance in this way under high competition stress. Therefore you should consider what proportion of time you should devote to the enhancement of technical development, and what proportion you should allocate to skill maintenance. There is, of course, no easy answer to this question, since it depends on the relative skill levels possessed by the performer under consideration. However, three factors may assist you:

1 If you devote 50 per cent of your training time to each aspect of skill, you will be attaching equal importance to them in terms of their overall contribution to competition performance.

2 Arguably, very few coaches devote enough time to developing the necessary skills to maintain performance.

3 Skill maintenance skills can be used during training just as much as during competition. Furthermore, this should lead to more efficient, effective learning, and therefore to improved technical development.

Whatever proportion of time you decide to spend on each aspect of training, you will still have to determine how to vary those proportions through the training period. During a period of general preparation for competition, it would seem logically appropriate to try to spend an equal portion of each session on the development of each aspect of skill. However, during preparation for a specific competition it is obviously inappropriate to try to enhance the maintenance of specific technical performance before it is fully developed. Therefore it is probably most effective to devote the whole of the first half of a pre-competition period to the development of technical skill, and the whole of the second half to maintaining that skill in the competitive environment. For example, an ice dancer might spend the first half of the pre-competition period learning new moves, and the second half putting together a routine and practising it under increasing external stress.

Perhaps the most important thing to remember about skill maintenance training is that it must be structured in such a way that the performer can *measure* his progress towards his competition goals. Also, since self-confidence has been shown to be an important determinant of performance, the outcomes of these learning experiences should almost always be positive. Thus, skill maintenance training is related to goal-setting. The goals which have been set must be achievable within the time allocated, so that self-confidence can be enhanced. The improvement which will result from this performance accomplishment can then be used to set more difficult goals for subsequent competitions.

However, a word of warning is also in order regarding such increases in goal-difficulty. Because of the shape of the curve which relates performance to goal-difficulty (see page 43), moderate increases in goal-difficulty will produce only small improvements in performance as the optimal level is approached; but big increases in goal-difficulty are likely to take the performer beyond his goal acceptance limit and lead to a large decrease in performance.

Finally, do not over-maintain really well-learned skills. In an attempt to achieve perfection in such skills, you may be tempted continually to draw your performer's attention to small details of performance that require modification. Understandably, many performers find this sort of approach quite disheartening. Some positive reinforcement is necessary to maintain even a well-learned response. In fact, the literature recommends a reinforcement ratio of 1:4; that is, one positive reinforcement at some stage for every four "correct" responses. Since you, the coach, are one of your performer's prime sources of reinforcement, this is worth bearing in mind. Of course, your performers should also be encouraged to reinforce their own "correct" responses for themselves, so that they are not totally dependent upon you in this respect.

On the day

What to say and what not to say

Many coaches see one of their major responsibilities as being to "psych up" their performers on the day. However, there are huge differences in the way individuals like to approach competitions. Some like to congregate and talk, while others prefer to sit quietly alone and think; some prefer to arrive at the competition site early to wander about to get the "feel" of it, while others prefer to arrive as late as possible, get changed, and go straight into action. Furthermore, the same performer's approach may vary from day to day and from competition to competition. Consequently, what will "psych up" one performer will quite definitely "psych" another performer right out! Get to know each of your performers' likes and dislikes in this respect; and, when they arrive at the competition site, try to get some sort of feel for how they would like to approach that particular competition. Usually, this will require you to listen to your performers rather than talking to them or directly questioning them.

On the day of any big competition, most performers will feel at least some anxiety or worry about the outcome. As we have already indicated, when people feel like this they automatically tend to seek support which will help them to cope and reduce their apprehension. In particular, when they look at you, their coach (the "one who knows the answers"), they are not likely to be reassured if they see you nervously pacing up and down, chain-smoking, or doing any of the other things you do when you are very anxious! Try to be at ease, behave normally, and at least look as if you are in control of the situation. This may sound easy enough, but it is actually something that most coaches find very difficult to do.

Consider this true example of a gymnast who was suffering from competitive anxiety: the gymnast's coach had realised the importance of not being too critical near a competition, and so had adopted a strategy of "watch and say nothing" at competitions. However, this was so unlike his "everyday" coaching style (which was very enthusiastic and forthright), that the gymnast in question interpreted the silence as indicating that the coach was annoyed and criticizing him. Not unnaturally, he therefore started to worry about how he was going to perform, and usually did perform very badly, by his own standards, as a result. The problem was not solved until the coach learned how to make an objective assessment of his *own* behaviour at competitions. It took some time!

Of course, in certain sports it is possible for the coach to offer a great deal of support to his performers when they are struggling during their competition. Performers continually receive information about the outcomes of their actions. Quite apart from its direct influence on future information processing, such feedback can also influence motivational aspects of performance, as shown in Figure 5.2. In some sports, the performer has to handle these problems for himself, as the coach is allowed no contact once the competition has started (e.g. rugby, judo, athletics). However, in others the coach has regular opportunities to talk to the performer and influence his motivational state and future decision-making (e.g. gymnastics, basketball, football). In particular, the coach can use verbal persuasion to greatly reduce, or remove, the effects of failure feedback on self-confidence, provided that he is sensitive and can "read" his performers. For example, you must learn to recognize the symptoms which indicate that *your performer* (not just you) has perceived feedback as indicating failure. In some cases a simple distraction away from the failure feedback may stop your performer from even noticing that a failure has occurred. Conversely, of course, telling him not to worry about it may only serve to draw his attention to it

Warming up mentally

In just the same way as we must warm up physiologically before strenuous

56

exercise, so we must also warm up mentally before psychologically demanding tasks. It is because of this fact that when we start to perform a task it takes a few trials for the required activation pattern to be established and the best performance to be attained. This period of "tuning in" can be greatly reduced if the performer practises an activity requiring a similar activation pattern immediately before the performance.

In most sports, performers do get the opportunity to warm up in this way immediately before they have to compete, but in others they are prevented from doing so. This *warm-up decrement*, as it is called, presents quite a serious problem. For example, in gymnastics performers may have to sit down for up to 30 minutes following a 2-minute warm-up before they are required to perform technically difficult and sometimes dangerous routines. Similarly, ski racers, canoeists, boxers and ice-skaters must all enter their competitive environment "cold".

Fig. 5.2 Path diagram showing some of the motivational influences on performance

Fortunately, there is some evidence to suggest that in such situations mental rehearsal (imagery) of the task(s) to be performed can help to reinstate the appropriate activation pattern. This is particularly the case if mental rehearsal has been used regularly in combination with varied physical practice of the tasks in question during training (see pages 45–47).

Properly structured warm-ups can also combat the effects of anxiety by reinstating an appropriate activation pattern and improving self-confidence. The basic idea here is a fairly commonsense one. If the warm-up is structured in such a way that the performer starts with easy tasks and *gradually* attempts more and more difficult ones, then at each stage his performance accomplishment, and therefore his self-confidence, will also increase (see page 41).

After the event

Handling success and failure

After any serious competition it takes some time for the system to "warm down" and readjust to the demands of a

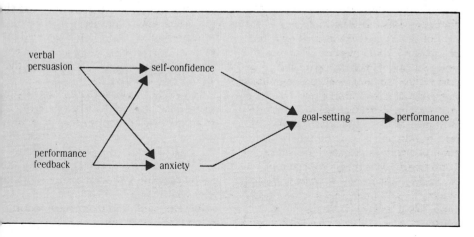

normal environment. Psychologically, this period is used by the performer to relax and reset his activation pattern for normal everyday life. Some performers are much better able to do this than others. They are usually referred to as having a *flexible style of attention*, that is to say, they can reset their activation patterns from one task to another very quickly. The American golfers Lee Trevino and Jack Nicklaus, for example, probably lie at opposite ends of this personality trait. Trevino appears to maintain a "normal" activation pattern for as long as possible during a competition, adjusting his activation pattern to golf only for the brief period of time necessary to play a shot. Nicklaus, on the other hand, seems to keep his activation pattern adjusted to golf for the whole of the competition period, apparently brooding between shots rather than engaging in normal social behaviour. Some of your performers too will require a long time after their competitions before they are able to engage in normal social behaviour and probably much longer before they are able objectively to evaluate and discuss their performance. During this time, the best thing you can do is to be discreet, but generally supportive of their performance.

The most appropriate time to start objectively evaluating performance is probably about 1–2 days after the competition has finished. You should discuss generally with the performer to what extent his goals were achieved. In particular, look at the question of whether the goals were set at a realistic enough level to give the performer a good chance of achieving them, and at a high enough level for their achievement to give him genuine satisfaction. Future goals should then be adjusted where necessary.

You should also try to decide whether or not any goal-setting "contracts" have been broken. Usually, broken contracts are accompanied by one of two outcomes: either the original goals are not achieved, or they are achieved but the performer demonstrates little or no satisfaction with his performance. It is theoretically possible for a performer to accept his goal right through performance, and then feel dissatisfied afterwards because this goal was achieved too easily. However, it is much more common for this situation to occur because goals have been rejected and replaced by more difficult ones before the performer has arrived at the competition site. Whatever the cause of these situations, the frustration which accompanies such experiences can do little to motivate the performer positively for future competitions. There is no universal solution to the problem of performers persistently breaking contracts, although the following approaches may help:

- Have performers set written goals which are then publicly displayed on a notice board. This makes the contract seem more binding, particularly if the performer also keeps his own written copy of the contract.
- Set goals during competition training when the performer is already under a fair amount of competitive stress.
- Make a qualitative change to the type of goal which is set.

Consider the case of a performer who had very high achievement motivation coupled with high levels of anxiety, and who continually under-achieved in competition. This performer would usually "give up" during the second half of competitions, despite the fact that he was actually performing quite well. Eventually, it emerged that this "quitting" was brought about by broken goal-setting contracts, since it appeared that the performer increased the difficulty of his goals as he gradually achieved them in training (this presumably related to his intense desire to succeed—high achievement motivation). When he got to competitions he failed to achieve these high goals because of his anxiety. In an attempt to remedy this situation, the coach changed his goals from "scores" to proving that he was not a "quitter". It was suggested to him that even very good performers make mistakes, but the difference between them and performers who were not quite so good was that the very good performer always bounced straight back after such a mistake. Consequently, he should view any mistakes which he might make as good, since they would give him the opportunity to prove that he had what it took to be a really good performer, whereas without any mistakes there could always be a question mark about his ability to recover from them. Of course, if he made two mistakes, he could regard this as even better, since only truly great performers could recover from such a situation! In his next competition, despite poor preparation due to injury, this performer represented his country in his first ever full international, and performed flawlessly throughout the competition!

Coach—performer relationships

It is probably obvious to most coaches that good coaches and good performers require different psychological attributes. For example, a top-class performer must be determined and single-minded to the point of selfishness, while a top coach must be analytical and flexible in his approach to both people and problems. However, what is perhaps not quite so obvious is that the functional differences between coaches and performers can produce severe conflict between them. For example, it has been shown that performers generally attribute failure to external influences (like bad refereeing, the weather, the track, etc.), while coaches generally attribute failure to internal causes within the control of the performer. Furthermore, even in success there is conflict, since it has also been shown that performers—not surprisingly—attribute success almost entirely to themselves, while coaches at best attribute it to the coach-performer interaction, and at worst attribute it almost entirely to themselves! Such situations clearly need delicate handling, particularly immediately after the completion of a competition.

Was your coaching effective?

Finally, if it is appropriate for your performers to set goals which can be objectively assessed, then it is clearly also important for you to set such behavioural goals for yourself. The problem is, how do you assess your own goal achievement? Perhaps the easiest way to do this is to have a video recording made of yourself both during training and during competition. With careful goal-setting and later analysis of the recording, you will learn a great deal about yourself. It isn't just performers who say "Did I really do that?"!

The last comment quite nicely raises the point that coaches are themselves performers who need continuously to plan, execute and evaluate their own performance. If you review the earlier chapters of this book, and apply all that has been said about learning and performing to your own performance as a coach, then you should achieve two things. First, you will demonstrate to yourself how well you understand what has been said; and, second, you ought to be able to identify where and how you might improve your performance as a coach. After all, you should now see why we have argued that coaching is about coaches learning as much as it is about performers learning.

Chapter 6
Match Analysis

Introduction

Paralleling the growth of interest in coaching, there has been a noticeable increase in the presentation of "match facts" in the media over the past few years, ranging from basic tables of soccer goalscorers in the newspapers to complex cricket-stroke indicators on Australian television. This kind of information has many uses, from historical record-keeping to sports coaching.

"Popular statistics" can be useful to coaches, but more often than not they give an over-simplified picture which can be misleading: the aim of this chapter is to give coaches some idea of how to use existing match-analysis systems—and, more importantly, how to set up systems to serve the particular needs of their own sport situations.

Coaching is a deliberate act of intervention in sport with the intention of improving performance. The purpose of match analysis is to evaluate performance in order to inform the coaching process. This process involves a cycle of logical steps (see Figure 6.1), each of which is designed to cut down the uncertainty a performer will meet in competition. For example, fitness schedules should meet the precise demands of the sport contest, technique practices should equip performers with an appropriate repertoire for the tasks they face, and so on.

One of the best starting points in the coaching process is analysis of individual competitive performance or of team performance in specific events. Since the coach's aim is to improve on existing performance, s/he must first watch the match in order to collect relevant information, then analyse the information to produce a plan which is implemented in practice sessions. Planning and practising involve interaction between coach and player(s), but the responsibility for observing and analysing must lie with the coach, if for

Fig. 6.1 Scheme of the coaching process

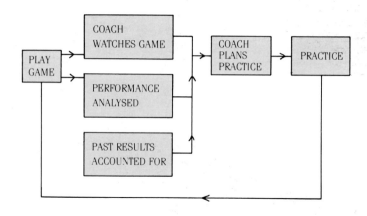

no other reason than that the players are otherwise engaged!

Depending on the sophistication of the analysis, subsequent coaching will be either better or worse. For example, while all coaches use their eyes and memory to make "mental notes", most of these observations are normally forgotten or obscured. Coaches are not alone in this respect!

Many coaches have developed their own methods of recording and analysing sport. These are usually closely kept secrets—proof that sport coaches value the findings of match analysis!

Four major *functions* of match analysis may be identified. These are:

Modelling

Modelling is simply the drawing-up of a complete "picture" of a particular sport. Just as an electrician needs a detailed and accurate wiring diagram in order to find faults in a system, so a coach should have an idea of what is expected and acceptable in certain situations: for example, errors are inevitable in sport, but what level of error is acceptable in, say, penalty-stroke taking in hockey, or in catching passes in rugby football?

Teams and individual players may demonstrate stereotypicality—in other words, a habitual way of playing. These stereotypes or profiles are also models, but *idiosyncratic models* which can include both good and bad sport habits. Match analysis reveals these habits as well as identifying the "game syntax" or tactical grammar which typifies a team or individual.

Compiling the facts to enable us to build models of sport is a long job, but experience suggests that, after about ten matches, some patterns of play begin to emerge and stabilise. Once a model is established, it can be used as a baseline for comparison with single

performances. A coach might want to compare performance across seasons, or against the same opponents at different times.

Although many coaches will not be directly involved in the actual construction of models, their cooperation is needed for identifying the most important aspects of play and for the collection of basic data.

Post mortems

The most obvious function of match analysis is to provide the coach with food for thought after a competition. This can then be used as a stimulus to alter strategy, introduce remedial training or to reinforce what has been successful—it is just as important to point out when performance is good, as to identify the problems!

Selection

Player selection is one of the most controversial procedures in sport, especially in those sports which involve teamwork and/or high levels of subjective judgement. Match analysis can be used to provide objective appraisal of player performance, and thereby to supplement (but never replace) the intuitive reasoning of selectors.

Scouting

Few coaches in British sport have the time to scout extensively, either for talent-spotting or for appraising opponents. However, it is possible to use match analysis as a scouting tool, once again to back up subjective opinions. By making scouting methods more objective in this way, they might well become a more worthwhile investment.

Do not imagine that this information has to be kept in elaborate or expensive equipment, or gathered all at once. Simple card-index systems can be built up over the years, itemising individual player information and patterns of play used by the opposition. For example, all the player contacts with the ball can be plotted to give a rough chart of the load and range of work done by an individual in a match. Figure 6.2 shows an example of just such a *record card*: it highlights individual weaknesses and strengths for reference in future encounters, such as right/left preferences, favourite shots, susceptibility to fatigue, close marking, pressure and so on.

Fig. 6.2 Opponent record card for women's lacrosse

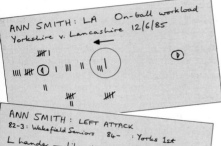

Perhaps the most astounding collection of match facts is that on soccer, compiled from over 2,000 games by an accountant, Charles Reep, over a thirty-year period. This has since been used as a database by the Football Association in devising their current coaching strategy (Hughes, 1984). The analysis focussed on the number of passes in possessions, and in particular the location and number of passes preceding attempts at goal.

Other hobbyists have collected match statistics in different sports, but few have turned their findings into coaching strategy with such conviction.

Why do coaches need match analysis?

The human eye-brain system is an unrivalled device for reasoning and problem-solving but it is unfortunately limited in its capacity for observation and recall. Because of the limitations of eyes, ears, attention span, concentration and memory, it is difficult for the coach to observe a match accurately and objectively. Without some access to backup storage, most of the events noticed by the brain are either forgotten or become distorted over a period of time.

Even experienced coaches may overlook key details of performance from time to time. For example, research on memory capacity among trained sport teachers and top coaches indicates that a specialist is only marginally better able to recall match information than a casual observer (Franks & Goodman, 1985). These findings support other studies, such as those on accident witnesses, which show that people miss a great deal of potentially important information when trying to watch relatively complex behaviour.

It can thus be seen that coaching will profit from the use of systems of recording match information that are more effective than simply watching and then remembering highlights.

The quality of both *watching* and *analysing* is crucial to the success of the coaching process. Not only must match information be comprehensively stored, but it should also be as objectively compiled as possible. For a host of reasons, it is very easy for unintended bias to creep into a coach's appraisal of a performance. In addition, competitors themselves invariably respond best to match records which have been objectively compiled and analysed.

Anyone can record observations of sports events, but *accurate* records can only be collected by trained observers using systems which have been carefully designed and refined in the match setting. Like any sport skill, match recording and analysis needs to be practised. Coaches need not necessarily be involved in the actual job of recording, but they should be able to understand the system, and even advise on how it should be set up and introduced; and they should certainly be able to interpret the results.

What do coaches want to know?

All sports have both technical and tactical dimensions, giving rise to different kinds of coaching knowledge and questions. For example, the tactical complexity of basketball is far greater than that of a track sprint, and the technical complexity of a pommel-horse routine is greater than that of freestyle swimming.

Different sports make different demands on performers in respect of techniques and tactics. In the past, the emphasis of coaching in the athletic (energy-testing) and gymnastic (movement-copying) sports has been mainly on technique. Even in games (territorial contests), where strategic possibilities are boundless, surprisingly little has been written on strategy compared with the volumes published on *how* to perform the various techniques. A good match-analysis system will help you to devise and exploit new strategic aspects of your sport.

While the recording of technical events is relatively easy, since techniques can be seen physically, the tactics of performance must be inferred because they exist only as plans in the performer's head. Match analysis is a

particularly useful aid for this tactical part of the coach's work.

The strategic component of athletic sports is often limited to race plans or single decisions, such as choosing the point of entry in jumping or weight-lifting contests. In gymnastic sports, strategic planning occurs prior to competition, with the coach taking a major role in choreographing the sequence of movements.

The games coach, on the other hand, can rehearse various strategic options with players but cannot "program" them because of the greater number of contingencies in games: indeed, part of the attraction and challenge of games lie in the demand for immediate responses induced by the opposition's actions. For this reason, all the examples given here are from the "fights and games" category of sport.

Particular difficulties arise when trying to analyse interactive games. Up to thirty people may be moving at once, and the off-ball play may be just as vital as play on the ball, if not more so. This problem can only be overcome by assigning one observer to each player and, although this has been attempted by some coaches, results are very difficult to collate. For now, we have to content ourselves with match-analysis methods which focus on the pathway of the ball.

Analysis methods

Match-analysis methods range from the very simple to the highly complex. The coach must first decide what s/he wants to know and this then determines the type of system which should be used. The use of technology does not necessarily make the analysis more difficult or sophisticated— it may indeed tell us less than we can see for ourselves. But technology can often improve the efficiency, depth or speed of analysis and is therefore at least worth consideration.

Pencil and paper records

Pencil and paper records have been used by generations of coaches, bench players and interested spectators, usually to produce player statistics. Typically, these involve the identification of key features of play which are recorded by the use of frequency tallies (see Figure 6.3). Summary totals can then be calculated and compared with previous figures statistically, graphically or by simple visual inspection.

Pencil and paper methods are quick and cheap, but they can really only be used effectively for sampling unless a commentator/observer works with a scribe, otherwise events are usually missed as the recorder's head moves up and down. In cricket, however, the pace of play is sufficiently slow for one person to record the events, and Bill Frindall's score books have come to represent perhaps the most widely known example of sport records. The major disadvantage of this system is that you get a *record* but no *analysis*. Subsequent analysis of a

Fig. 6.3 Assessing goal achievement in competition

Player: Pele   Assessor: Joe Soap

ON THE BALL	Player receives ball with good control	Accurate passes	Dribbles past an opponent	Shots or headers on target	Player loses the ball through poor control	Inaccurate passes	Loses ball dribbling in first ⅔ of field	Loses ball dribbling in final ⅓ of field	Shots or headers off target
First half	LHT LHT LHT H	LHT LHT 1	LHT 1	1111					11
Total									
Second half									
Total									

OFF THE BALL	Player makes himself readily available	Players create space for another player	Player gets into opponent's penalty area	Player adopts position in an inappropriate zone of the field					
First half	LHT LHT LHT LHT	LHT 111	LHT LHT LHT 1111	LHT LHT LHT 1111					
Total									
Second half									
Total									

match usually requires several hours, and has been known to take days!

Perhaps the most frequently seen player statistics are those displayed on screen by American television during coverage of tennis. These show, for example, the number of first serves in, and/or aces served by each player. Similarly, Channel 4's coverage of volleyball gives information on serving, control of service, blocking and smash/dump success rates. Although these details are presented for the interest of spectators, they can also be useful to coaches.

Example 1: Data was collected on a pro basketball squad's league games over a whole season (Kemp, 1985). Figure 6.4 shows selected information on shooting, although turnovers and rebounds were noted as well. In this squad the three imported North American players, numbers 6, 11 and 14, are the principal attackers of the basket with over 400 attempts each. Their success rates are 55, 54 and 59 per cent respectively, comparing well with other teams in the league. The best English player, no. 8, makes almost 300 attempts on the basket, but his success rate is only 43 per cent, well down on the others and below the average figure for both the team as a whole and their collective opponents. Here, it is the coach's job to interpret the findings and act upon them.

This kind of data is a summation of performance over a period of time, records being kept on a match-by-match basis. It has been the practice in basketball for many years to keep tallies of fouls and other match events: statistical ("stat") sheets are commercially available for this purpose and are now also used in some other sports such as lacrosse. Information like

Number	Games Played
4	25
5	3
6	26
7	24
8	26
9	19
10	25
11	26
12	3
13	5
14	26
15	26
HS	26
OP	26

Technique	A
Raw Data:	
1 ENGLAND	30
2 OPPONENTS	55
3 TOTAL	85
Percentages:	
4 ENGLAND	4
5 OPPONENTS	8
6 TOTAL	6

this allows the coach and players to monitor shooting success rates for both field goals and free throws as the season progresses, and thus it can be used to assess current form, to set targets for improvement and to justify selection choices.

The production of a permanent paper record of match events requires the use of a system of *notation*. Such systems can

| | Shots | | | Free Throws | | Total | Game |
Made	Attempted	%	Made	Attempted	%	Points	Average
8	22	36	0	1	0	16	1
0	1	0	0	0	0	0	0
228	417	55	65	74	88	580	22
56	111	50	22	28	79	148	6
126	292	43	21	31	68	280	11
0	2	0	0	0	0	0	0
6	12	50	0	0	0	12	0
277	516	54	70	95	74	641	25
8	21	38	3	9	33	19	6
14	34	43	3	4	75	31	6
251	429	59	33	61	54	545	21
47	78	60	2	3	67	97	4
		53			70		90
		51			73		94

Fig. 6.4 Player statistics for a pro basketball squad

B	C	D	E	F	G	H	TOTAL
142	19	56	51	414	62	42	816
170	17	69	60	212	77	42	702
312	36	125	111	626	139	84	1518
17	2	7	6	51	8	5	100
24	2	10	9	30	11	6	100
21	2	8	7	41	9	6	100

Fig. 6.5 Frequency analysis of karate techniques

be very simple, or may be elaborated to rival the complex forms of notation devised for recording choreographic dance compositions. Notation is useful for providing quickly stored and easily translated records: it comprises symbols recorded in various formats, often vertical or horizontal linear layouts, in grids or on charts. About 6 to 8 hours of practice is needed to become reasonably competent with a basic notation system. Head movements while attempting to observe and record simultaneously can again cause a sampling problem unless some intermediate store of events is made using video or audiotape.

Example 2: A notation system can be

used to ask general questions about the nature of performance in a given sport. In a recent study of karate all the moves used by fighters in an international competition were notated using paper and pencil (see Figure 6.5 for a breakdown of moves). Symbols were invented to denote the twelve single or combination techniques in this form of karate.

In all, 1521 technical moves were recorded: two of the techniques taught by coaches were *not used at all* in the competition; a third technique was used only once and a fourth only twice. In the latter two cases the techniques did not score. An astute coach might ask why these techniques survive in the training repertoire and might make adjustments to future coaching sessions on the basis of such results.

Example 3: A netball coach (Potter, 1985) was interested to compare the pathway of the ball after the centre pass in schoolgirl games with the pathway advocated in the coaching books. Having numbered each player and divided the court into nine areas, she was able to chart the centre pass possessions by player and area.

The text book said that scoring opportunities should result from direct attacks down the centre of the court using possessions of only 3 or 4 passes,

including the centre pass. In this study, the squad showed a tendency to veer to the right side of the court (see Figure 6.6) despite having been coached to use the centre route. This analysis raises the question of whether the team should in fact be coached to attack down the centre, since this was not their most successful route.

Video

An attractive alternative to pencil and paper recording is to make a visual record of the match in order to allow it to be viewed more than once, and if necessary, in slow motion. With the advent of relatively cheap and portable videotape hardware, video has become widely adopted for match analysis and has largely superseded the use of film. Video enables a complete record of the event to be made and analysed conveniently at leisure.

Even so, problems can still arise; for example, video equipment is still beyond the budget of some sport organisations; identification of individual players is sometimes difficult and the field of vision of the camera may cause some features of play to be missed. A reliable power supply is needed and a stable platform must be found. Sliding tracks or tripods can be used, although these may restrict the camera angle to a certain extent.

Fig. 6.6 Analysis of centre pass attacks in netball

Route	Left	Centre	Right	Total
Positive	14	35	52	**101**
Negative	15	43	23	**81**
Total	**29**	**78**	**75**	**182**

Analysis of the tape itself is a time-consuming business, since the features of interest to the coach must be distilled and the observer is just as susceptible to "highlighting" as when live matches are watched.

Despite these difficulties, almost all top-level coaches now use video matches at some point in their training programmes. The psychological value of video and the reality of its images make it a powerful means of motivating players when compared with tables or charts generated from notation.

Audiotape

Audiotape has the advantages of allowing a complete record to be made of those events which the coach pre-selects, and, if a microtape is used, of freeing the observer/recorder to move about during the competition and get the best possible view. Batteries should always be tested before the start of the event and spares kept to hand!

The drawback with this method is the amount of time it takes to get the information from the tape into a digestible form—perhaps 4 to 8 hours for a single match. However, systems are rapidly being developed to allow the audiotaped features of play to be typed directly into a computer keyboard. This cuts analysis time down to roughly the length of the live game itself.

Example 4: The BRACSTAT system of notation (Brackenridge & Alderson, 1983) has been used with lacrosse, hockey, basketball and soccer. The resulting transcription is read rather like a musical score and gives a permanent record which can be consulted in subsequent seasons or compared with past performances. Very little practice is necessary to read the flow of play, although at first glance the overall effect

may appear rather daunting!

The columnar arrangement shows details of both teams' possessions, and allows key aspects of the match to be picked out at a glance. It can be used to tally various features of play such as goals, shots and tackles, and to identify patterns of play from the path of the ball. Remember, you follow the movement of the ball by reading from top to bottom of the columns. The following exercise will make you familiar with the system.

To show how the method is built up, we have devised an imaginary game in the simple sport of "Binball". There are five players in each team, any of whom may score by getting the ball into the opposing colour's bin.

The teams

| Red: | 1 | 2 | 3 | 4 | 5 |
| Blue: | A | B | C | D | E |

There is no hard and fast rule about identifying the players: use whatever method suits *you*, such as numbers on shirts, or initials if you know the players really well.

The court is divided into six areas (see Figure 6.7).

Fig. 6.7 Binball court

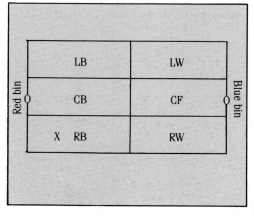

These areas are designated as follows:

RB = Right Back
LB = Left Back
CB = Centre Back
RW = Right Wing
LW = Left Wing
CF = Centre Forward

On this court the actual areas are imaginary: also they are labelled according to which team is in possession at the moment. So, if the Reds are playing from left to right, the area with the X in it is RB for them, but becomes LW as soon as the Blues get the ball! Sounds confusing? Don't be put off: it is only an extention of how most of us think during team play, and the necessary mental switch each time possession changes quickly becomes quite automatic. The advantage over the obvious alternative of permanently labelling the areas is that the transcription you end up with is much more easily interpreted.

REDS v. BLUES 29/4/87 PAGE 1

SCORE	R	B	SCORE	R	B	SCORE	R	B
0-0	T						8 CB	5 RW
	2 CF						C RB	4 CF
	3 RW						E RW	S+
	4 CF					3-1	8 CF	T
	1 LW						A CB	PLAY CONTINUES
	2 CF						D LW	:
	Sx						B CF	
		B CB					S+	
		C RW						
		x	2-1	T				
	2 CF				4 LW			
	3 RB				5 CF			
	5 RW				Sx			
	S+				B CB			
1-0	T				E CF			
	2 CF				C RW			
	5 RW				D LW			
	3 RW				Sx			
	4 LW				2 CB			
	1 CF				1 LB			
	2 CF				x			
	S+				2 CB			
2-0	T				1 LB			

Fig. 6.8 Sample notation of a binball match

The symbols

T = Tip-off, to start or re-start play
x = Incomplete pass
Sx = Missed shot at goal
S+ = Goal!

With only these basic details, plus a supply of suitably ruled paper, we can build up the picture of the first few minutes of play as shown in Figure 6.8.

The result gives a much greater amount of information than might be thought at first glance:

Passes—every time one player appears directly above another, it denotes a pass.

Passing errors—these show up as a small "x" beside the receiver, followed usually by a change of possession!

Ratio of conversion—a measure of the effectiveness of a team: find it by dividing the number of passes a team makes by the number of goals it scores.

Possession—shows up each time a player or sequence of players appears in the team's column, and ends on a turnover or goal.

Average length of passing sequence—this is established by totalling the number of a team's passes and dividing the result by the number of passing "strings".

The *number of passes leading to a shot at goal* is found simply by locating each "S" symbol and counting back from it.

Assists are as almost as important as accurate shots. From the notation you can pick out the area from which the pass was made which led to a shot, and also the player who made it.

Goals—each "S +" is a goal: by looking back from them you can see who scored, who assisted, where from, and how many passes led to it.

See if you can work out the answers to the following questions by studying the transcript. Check your answers with those given at the end of this chapter.

1 Who gave the most passes on each team?

2 What proportion of passing errors was committed by each team?

3 What was the ratio of conversion for each team?

4 How many possessions did each team have?
(Possession ends on a turnover or goal)

5 What was the average length of passing sequence?
(Sequence ends on a fumble or goal)

6 How many passes preceded each shot at goal?

7 From which area on court were the assists given?

8 From which area on court were the goals scored?

Once you have got the hang of the simple notation for "Binball", it is easy to modify it to suit more complex games. You will soon develop symbols appropriate to the needs of your particular sport, e.g. for throw-ins, dribbles, corner kicks, etc.

Computer systems

Several match analysts have developed systems which utilise an on-line computer facility. This requires a mains electricity supply plus protection from the elements, but has the great advantage of providing almost instant feedback to the coach and players. Honeywell have recently supplied minicomputer facilities to the BBC for test match coverage of cricket, but the traditional cricket statisticians are only just beginning to experiment with computers.

In the USA such systems have become so sophisticated that they have been banned at pro football games! The ethical issues arising from this remain to be discussed in the United Kingdom, but we have a long way to go before we can claim technological parity with North America.

Example 5: Franks *et al* (1983) configured a computer keyboard to resemble the layout of a soccer field and designed a program which yielded frequency tallies of various features of play. A video was time-locked to the system so that relevant sections of the match could be replayed visually alongside the computer analysis.

Typing match details into a conventional computer keyboard is only one way of inputting data. It can be laborious and, since mistakes are inevitable, programs must include error-trapping routines. Other input devices are available which will cut out certain stages in the procedure and might also eventually prove faster and more accurate.

One such device is the *concept keyboard*, a smooth-surfaced touch-sensitive pad on which any grid or diagram of the match area can be superimposed. The keyboard is connected to the computer so that merely touching its surface triggers an input. The potential of such a device for match analysis is exciting, but as yet only a few sport researchers have begun to explore its possibilities.

Another input device which coaches may eventually be able to adopt is the *voice analyser*. This can be programmed to recognise commands from one person's voice, and may therefore be used to bypass the audiotape stage of commentary on a match. It would feed directly into the computer for analysis and thus save considerable time and effort.

Although some coaches might find computers and electronic devices threatening or confusing, it should always be remembered that they are merely an additional aid to supplement the coach's own intuitive decisions about sport. They will become a regular part of the coach's armoury but can never replace a good coach!

It is likely that the coaches of the future will select from a range of match-analysis methods and may combine two or three to secure the best possible information for their particular sports. Pencil and paper methods will probably remain the most widely used recording system because they are cheap, convenient and flexible. However, the enterprising coach will explore other systems.

How to get started

Before adopting a particular system, each coach will need to examine carefully the demands of his/her particular sport and identify the key questions to be answered. A good meal is made from good ingredients, and a good match analysis comes from carefully selected parameters and intelligently interpreted results.

The system adopted should fit the needs of the coach, not vice versa, so coaching requirements will to some extent dictate the kind of system used. For example, if a coach wants to know about goal-mouth incidents in hockey s/he may use video rather than BRACSTAT since video shows the movements of all players simultaneously. If, on the other hand, a workload analysis of an individual player is required then a hand-drawn paper trace might be best, or, ideally, a concept-keyboard trace.

So, decide first *what* is wanted and then *how* to go about recording and analysing.

The next stage is to try out some simple grids and checklists to show the location and nature of the various features of play selected. For example, a list of cricket shots could be matched against a plan of the field to show where particular batsmen choose to play the ball.

Having experimented with a few ideas on paper and tried them out at matches, refine your system until you are satisfied that it is providing the information you require. It is useful to consult the players as they will be the recipients of your match-analysis feedback and should be able to understand exactly what you are doing and why you are doing it!

Other coaches may also help you to develop and interpret a system for your sport: even if you decide not to be involved in the actual process of collecting information it is vital that you are fully involved in the design or choice of your system.

Using match analysis

The hallmark of a good match-analysis system is user-friendliness. If a system is offputting or gives too much, too little or the wrong information then it is no good to the coach. One of the pitfalls of match analysis is what might be termed "information overkill"—giving too much detail which is guaranteed to saturate both the coach and the player.

To the cynics, match analysis may seem to be a long-winded way of finding out what the coach already knows. But most coaches have a genuine desire to learn more about their sport, and we now have enough evidence to convince even the cynics that match analysis has an important role to play in the coaching process.

The best of all possible worlds, of course, is to combine the knowledge, experience and intuitive judgement of the coach with the accuracy, objectivity and rigour of a good match-analysis system. In many sports we have yet to reach this stage.

Answers to analysis exercise

Red No: 2
Blue No: B

2 Red 1 out of 16
Blue 1 out of 10

3 Red 1: 5.3
Blue 1: 10

4 Red 5⎫
Blue 3⎭ = 8

5 $(27/8) = 3.38$

6

Shot	1	2	3	4	5	6	7
Passes	4	2	5	6	1	3	3

7

Assists	1	2	3	4
From	RB	CF	LW	RW

8

Goal	1	2	3	4
From	RW	CF	CF	CF

Chapter 7

What sort of Coach are you?

Knowing yourself

Task Try answering the following questions as honestly as you can. Write down your answers, so that you can come back to them later and think about them.

1 How do you coach at present? Do you intend to change your style or methods at all?

2 Can you ask yourself the right questions about your style, and give honest answers?

3 Do you lead by example, through your own standards of behaviour? Or is it a case of "Do as I say, not as I do"?

4 Are you observant—do you see what your performers *actually* do? Do you *hear* them when they have something to say?

5 Do you assess? Is your feedback to your performers factual, with information to help them change, or does it simply display your pleasure or displeasure?

6 Do you differentiate between *performance progress* and *effort*?

7 Do your performers learn by *trial and error*, or by *trial and error elimination*?

8 Do you shape their trials with positive reinforcement?

9 Are you aware of how your performer sees or perceives the task—the goal, the problem, or the activity? Are they trying to do what you think they are?

10 Are you aware of your performers' emotional state and their general emotional disposition towards the goals/tasks/problems which concern you and them together?

11 Do you put your performers' well-being ahead of your own ambitions for yourself, your team or your club?

It is important to notice that skilful performance depends upon many elements. Among these are:

FITNESS   TECHNIQUE
EMOTION   PERCEPTION
EQUIPMENT

These must all be improved if progress is to be made, but only your performer can change them. They are all interrelated, and you can help your performer to develop only when you are aware of these relationships.

What are the results of your coaching?

Do you evaluate your performers' progress? Try to:

- Keep a record of how your performers learn the techniques and skills of your sport.
- Record the physical changes that occur in your performers.
- Be aware of changes in their relationships with others.
- Know about the age-group standards or other standards in your sport.

- Notice whether your performers still *enjoy* taking part.
- Assess when and why they depend on you for support.

If you are effective as a coach, you will be a major influence on the total lifestyle of your performers. The nature of this influence will depend on your personality and theirs, but it should move towards a caring, stable and resourceful coaching relationship in which the performer is autonomous.

This relationship should lead to an appreciation of the roles of others involved in the structure of your sport, including officials, law-makers, committee members, sponsors and supporters.

Consider this quote from James Counsilman, the American swimming coach:

> The coach is an educated director of ... people who are striving for a goal. He must not drive them relentlessly, but should guide them intelligently towards this goal.

Fig. 7.1 Coaching styles

How do others see you?

Your style of coaching will largely be determined by your personality. It will vary from person to person and from time to time. It will change with each situation, and you will adapt your behaviour according to your performers' needs. There is no *one* way of coaching: indeed, you may find it necessary to adopt different approaches for different groups. At one end of the scale you may have to act in a very authoritarian, autocratic manner, whereas at the other extreme you may need to be unimposing and easy-going. There is thus a continuum of coaching styles, which need to be appreciated if you are to vary your "act" to suit your "audience".

The approach that falls somewhere between the two extremes is that of co-operative guidance. In the co-operative style you are the *guider*, or you are the *gardener*—recognizing that your performers are organic! The textbook still applies, but *apply* is the key word. This means that you do not abandon all the theory you have learned, but you adapt your approach to suit the individual. Each performer is different,

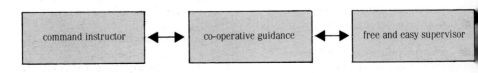

| command instructor | co-operative guidance | free and easy supervisor |

and only he or she can do the growing, learning and developing. You cannot do the growing for them; you can only help. How? As the gardener, you create the right environment—you will select, protect, "weed" occasionally, give improved nourishment, more or less sunlight or limelight, and determine suitable rates of growth. This does not mean to impose growth-rates: your performers need to be helped to grow at their own rate. Do not forget that sometimes it may be necessary to "transplant" a performer into a new setting before he will flourish.

- You can encourage growth with an increasing knowledge of the sport.
- You will aid the motivation of your performers as you learn to know them better and as you develop empathy with their goals—which you can then help them to set, change and structure.

Presenting information

Now you should focus your attention on the practical implications of the theoretical material we have looked at. Below are six key elements of effective instruction, together with some questions to help you analyse your coaching methods after each session.

1. Activity selection
- Was the activity you chose to present challenging to the group?
- Was it possible for the group to be successful?
- Are the performers making satisfactory progress?

2. Instruction
- Are the performers aware of the objects of the session?
- Did you present an appropriate model (demonstration) of the skill?

- Was the practice assisted by suitable feedback, with verbal, visual and kinesthetic cues emphasised?
- Did you allow the performers time to apply the skill in a game-like situation?
- Did you allow for individual differences between performers?

3. Participation
- Did you reduce your talking time to a minimum?
- Did you organize the group effectively?
- Did you give clear instructions for managing the equipment, thus facilitating smooth transitions?
- Did the practice situations you selected allow for as much participation by the group as possible?

4. Equal opportunity
- Did your method of instruction allow for left-handed (or left-footed) performers?
- Did you cater for the less able performers?
- Did you cater for other performers who were finding it hard to follow your teaching methods?
- Were your presentation techniques suitable for both male and female participants?

5. Safety
- Did you stress safety aspects as you presented the information?
- Did you follow the correct procedures when using equipment which can cause injury?
- Was all the equipment checked for its condition before using it?

6. Motivation
- Were the participants successful—that is, did you present the material in such a way that they

were enabled to achieve their
objectives?
- Did the group enjoy the session?
- Did you enjoy coaching them?

Index

W

Y